Au Revoir Angleterre

MAKING A GO OF MOVING ABROAD

Au Revoir Angleterre

MAKING A GO OF MOVING ABROAD

Paul Jenner & Christine Smith

EDITORS RICHARD CRAZE, RONI JAY

WHITE LADDER PRESS
new tricks for old dogs

Published by White Ladder Press Ltd
Great Ambrook, Near Ipplepen, Devon TQ12 5UL
01803 813343
www.whiteladderpress.com

First published in Great Britain in 2005

10 9 8 7 6 5 4 3 2 1

© Paul Jenner and Christine Smith 2005

The right of Paul Jenner and Christine Smith to be identified as authors of this work has been asserted by them in accordance with the Copyright, Designs and Patents Act 1988.

ISBN 0 9548219 0 4

British Library Cataloguing in Publication Data
A CIP record for this book can be obtained from the British Library.

All rights reserved. No part of this publication may be reproduced, stored in a retrieval system, or transmitted in any form or by any means, electronic, mechanical, photocopying, recording, or otherwise without either the prior written permission of the Publishers or a licence permitting restricted copying in the United Kingdom issued by the Copyright Licensing Agency Ltd, 90 Tottenham Court Road, London W1P 0LP. This book may not be lent, resold, hired out or otherwise disposed of by way of trade in any form of binding or cover other than that in which it is published, without the prior consent of the Publishers.

Designed and typeset by Julie Martin Ltd
Cover design by Julie Martin Ltd
Cover illustration by Sue Misselbrook
Printed and bound by TJ International Ltd, Padstow, Cornwall

White Ladder Press
Great Ambrook, Near Ipplepen, Devon TQ12 5UL
01803 813343
www.whiteladderpress.com

What other people have said about this book...

"*Au Revoir Angleterre* is realistic, extremely helpful and easy to read; a nice mixture of common sense and encouragement. Bravo! The book covers every basic question that a potential expatriate could reasonably ask." **Peter Mayle**

"I found this book to be humorous, true to life and terribly entertaining. It vividly reminded me of when I first arrived in France. I thought the opening questionnaire was particularly useful, and for anyone thinking of leaving the country this is a must have book."
John Burton Race

"Thinking of living the life of Riley in Sunshine Villa, Costa Nothing, Abroad? Read this wise and helpful book before you move, and give those dreams a reality check."
Christopher Somerville travel writer and journalist.

"Anyone who needs a change of scenery should read this book. A relocation manual for new-Europeans."
Nicholas Crane author of *Clear Waters Rising: A Mountain Walk Across Europe* (Penguin) and *Mercator, The Man Who Mapped the Planet* (Phoenix).

"*Au Revoir Angleterre* is a funny and practical look at the dream and reality of moving abroad. If everybody read it there would be no TV programmes about naive expats and their ruined dreams. I really enjoyed it. Essential reading."
Rosemary Bailey author of *Life In A Postcard – Escape to the French Pyrenees* (Bantam).

"Au Revoir Angleterre is thought provoking, informative and explains the hidden truths about living abroad. A MUST READ for every wannabe expat."
BritishExpats.com serving the expatriate community.

Contents

	Introduction	1
1	**Enjoying A Better Climate**	9
2	**Experiencing A Different Way Of Life**	16
3	**Life Will Somehow Be Better**	22
4	**A Less Stressful Pace Of Life**	27
5	**A Healthier Lifestyle**	33
6	**A Better Place To Bring Up Children**	39
7	**Life Will Be Cheaper**	45
8	**Enjoying Outdoor Sports**	52
9	**Making A New Start**	58
10	**Finding New Stimulation**	63
11	**An Affordable Dream Home**	68
12	**Being Near Sunny Beaches**	76

13	**Personal Growth**	81
14	**Restoring An Old Ruin**	87
15	**Becoming Fluent In Another Language**	94
16	**Being Near Ski Slopes**	100
17	**Retirement In The Sun**	106
18	**Romance**	112
19	**Living Among Like-Minded People**	118
20	**Foodie Heaven**	124
21	**Becoming A Real European**	130
22	**Becoming An Artist Or Writer**	136
23	**Living In The Wilderness**	142
24	**Having Your Own Olive Grove**	148

	What People Say About Living Abroad	154
	Conclusion	168
	Useful Contacts And Addresses	170

Introduction

A lot of people have been saying *Au revoir Angleterre* recently. Not to mention *Auf Wiedersehen Wales*. And *Adéu-siau Scotland*.

According to the latest official statistics 125,000 people are now leaving Britain every year to live permanently in other parts of the European Union (EU)[1]. And a similar number buy property in other EU countries for occasional use. These, remember, are only the official statistics. Given the lack of formalities required by many EU countries nobody can really know. The true figure is likely to be much higher.

About 25,000 move to cities (possibly sent by their employers) but the vast majority move either to the countryside or to coastal areas. In other words, they're making a lifestyle choice. These are the people this book is about. People, in all probability, just like you.

And the pace is accelerating. Affluence, the strong pound and high

---

[1] Office for National Statistics

Au Revoir Angleterre

property prices have all combined to make it possible. According to a recent investigation[2] one third of Britons are considering moving abroad to work or live.

For many the EU is the obvious choice, given its ideal of free movement. You can't just set up home in Australia or New Zealand or Canada whenever you wish but you can in France and Spain and Italy. Here's a nice game for your next dinner party. Ask your guests to name all 25 member countries. You'll probably be safe to make a little wager that they can't. Just to remind you, the EU now comprises: Austria, Belgium, Cyprus, the Czech Republic, Denmark, Estonia, Finland, France, Germany, Greece, Hungary, Ireland, Italy, Latvia, Lithuania, Luxembourg, Malta, the Netherlands, Poland, Portugal, Slovakia, Slovenia, Spain, Sweden and the UK.

It's sobering to think that at one time or another Britain has been at war with many of these countries. A very good reason for creating the EU. In fact, the influx of expats into some destinations could almost be described as an invasion but, thankfully, a peaceful one.

Are you going to join them? If you're reading this book you're obviously thinking about it. Here's a little quiz to see if you're the sort of person who would enjoy living abroad.

1. Would you really miss warm draught bitter, pickled onions, and paying before you drink – in other words, British pubs?
2. Do you ever watch (live or on TV): (a) The Queen's Christmas Message (b) The State Opening of Parliament (c) Wimbledon (d) any cricket matches?

[2] Alliance and Leicester International

Introduction

3   Have you recently installed fitted carpets and couldn't now imagine life without them?
4   Do you insist on: (a) Horlicks (b) Bovril (c) Marmite (d) custard (e) gravy (f) fish and chips (g) Weetabix?
5   Do you want a back garden (with a fence)?
6   Do you shop at Marks & Spencer: (a) daily (b) weekly (c) at least once a month?
7   Would you be miserable if it was sunny and warm on Christmas Day and Christmas lunch was served outside?
8   Do you regularly watch/listen to/read: (a) News at Ten (b) The Archers (c) a newspaper?

How did you get on?
- *Yes* to most questions – you'd better stay tucked up at home.
- A roughly equal number of *yesses* and *nos* – you'd be well advised to have a test run before committing yourself.
- Mostly *nos* – start packing.

Where will you go? Well, Spain is the most popular choice. Officially, you'd be joining just over 200,000 Brits already living there. But unofficially there are 700,000. Some observers even say one million. The French authorities talk of more than 350,000 British owned homes in France – but not necessarily occupied year round. Portugal has an estimated 200,000 British property owners. In other words, southern Europe. As one expat put it: 'Once you've tasted the south you can never go back.' From personal experience we'd say that's true.

It would help to know how those pioneers who went ahead of you made out. (Or maybe you've already gone and would just like to compare notes.) That's exactly the point of this book. We ran a survey to find out what people's top fantasies were. From that we designed a questionnaire to try to find out how the reality compared with the dreams. We interviewed more than a hundred expats. And we threw in a good dollop of our own experience from living abroad for more than 15 years, firstly in France and now in Spain. This book is the result.

In our case we eased our way gradually into living abroad. One winter, personal commitments and financial considerations came together to make it possible to spend three months skiing. We rented a house unseen (through an agency) and we were lucky. It was exactly our dream. An unspoilt agricultural village not far from a major ski station, smelling of cows and hay and wood smoke. We were thrilled. Once we'd tasted that, life could never be the same again.

The following winter we did the same thing, only this time for five months.

By the third winter there was, indeed, 'no going back'. We rented what was actually the most primitive barn of a place. In a town it would have been condemned as unfit for human habitation. In this tiny mountain village it was simply picturesque.

It was actually 10 years before we bought somewhere. During all that time we lived in a succession of rented homes in various villages on the French, and later the Spanish, side of the Pyrenees. This is a sensible way to start. It's a bit like trying on clothes before you decide to buy.

Certainly, it's never been easier to move to the mainland. Apart from the EU having swept away all kinds of bureaucratic hurdles, several other elements have come together.

Introduction

Cheap airlines have transformed the whole picture. Maybe you wouldn't contemplate living abroad because you have elderly parents who occasionally need help. Maybe you couldn't live abroad because your work requires you to be available for meetings in London. Now, suddenly, it's cheaper to commute into London once a week from Perpignan than it is from Manchester. It's crazy. But it's how it is. Suddenly it's possible to think of nipping back to Britain when your parents have problems (and they can just as easily slip out to see you). Suddenly it's possible to slip over to London once a month (or even once a week) to discuss projects. A few years ago it would all have been unthinkable.

Other marvellous developments are cheap phone calls and the internet. Ten years ago our telephone bill was astronomical because we needed to be on the phone to England every day. Now, with the same level of calls, we pay only a quarter of what we did then. That *is* amazing. And the internet means that, when necessary, we can send and receive contracts, drafts, sketches, designs, photographs and so on.

Looking at the responses we got to the survey, and from our own experience, certain things stand out. The first is that the vast majority of people are very pleased they made the move. Generally, the reality was not so very different from the dream. Of course, a few people do bitterly regret leaving the old country. And some go back. One man told us he had to give up the Balearics otherwise he would have died – of alcoholism. Well, that was him. Some expats do live that way.

The second is that people go abroad for rather vague reasons. In the companion volume *Out Of Your Townie Mind*, Richard Craze discovered that people move to the British countryside in pursuit of quite specific dreams. They mentioned things like going for long walks, growing their own vegetables, having open fires, keeping chickens and having roses round the door. People who go abroad, on the other hand, have a rather different mindset. They have a far bigger expectation of fundamental change. They dream that life will somehow be better, that they'll be subject to less stress, that they'll be healthier, that they'll make a new start and above all that they'll be *enjoying a better climate*. Of course, some of these goals are also shared by urban refugees in the British countryside but few expats drew on the kind of detailed images that the new-rurals did. They felt life would be better abroad *without really knowing why*. Basically, they just fell in love with the whole *romance* of living abroad.

Hopefully, when you've finished reading this book you'll have a better idea of the dreams that will be valid *for you*. The top 24 are presented in order of popularity. We've thrown quite a few pails of cold, wet scepticism at every one of them. Because we want you to go abroad with your eyes open and make a success of it.

But the truth is that, personally, we're not very sceptical at all. To us, living in France, and now Spain, never was a big deal. We never thought of it as a great, frightening ABROAD. There really is very little difference between living in Britain and living in France or Spain or Portugal or Italy or Greece. You name it. While some Brits are arguing about the euro and the constitution and all the rest of it, others (the Europhiles) are quietly packing up and leaving to join us.

Maybe we're in a minority but we *love* the EU. We used to live in a

Introduction

tiny little country. It was called Britain. Now we live in a place that stretches from inside the Arctic Circle to the Mediterranean, and from the Atlantic to the Aegean. We live in a place that contains some of the world's greatest mountain ranges, mightiest rivers and most ancient and fascinating cities. Oh, it's also worth mentioning that the weather in the southern part is vastly different from the northern part.

And a United States of Europe just can't come fast enough. Why? Because we're still a very long way from the freedom of movement that was one of the goals. Can you, for example, continue with your British driving licence or will you need a new licence from your adopted country? If you've got a foreign licence what happens when you go back to the UK on business? Can you transfer your British no-claims bonus to an insurance company abroad? What happens about health insurance? Can you still go back to Britain for NHS treatment – after all, you paid for it for years? Unemployment benefit? Supposing you only want to spend part of the year abroad, where do you pay tax? Supposing one year you spend four months in Spain, four months in France and four months in the UK? It's still all so horribly complicated. Basically, the EU still isn't set up for the substantial number of people who are now truly European.

That's how we think of ourselves. Not as British. Or Spanish. But as Europeans. To us it's our dream. And our reality.

To us it seems bizarre to live somewhere simply because – through no fault of your own – you were born there. That was just an accident. Why base your whole life on something over which you had no control rather than on the more logical process of selecting a location based on your personality, desires and ambitions?

Au Revoir Angleterre

But how? You have a career. Debts. Children. You don't speak any foreign languages. Well, other people in the same position have done it. They had their dreams and they made them come true. And don't forget that abroad is only an everyday, normal, bland experience to the people born there. Most of them are not rich, either.

Good luck!

Enjoying a better climate

— The Dream —

It's Christmas day. But, for you, there's no slumping in front of the television after a stodgy Christmas lunch, the stuffy central heating on at full blast, while the gloom deepens outside. Lunch will be on the terrace. For now you take a few minutes to relax, sitting in your shorts beside the swimming pool. It's not hot — no more than about 20°C — but the sun is beating down from a clear blue sky with such intensity that you can almost feel your skin turning brown. After lunch you and your partner may saddle your horses and trot down to the river, or maybe jump in the sports car, top down, and drive to the tennis club. You reach for the portable telephone to wish the folks back in England a Merry Christmas. And what's the weather like back there? Cold, eh? Raining? Grandad's suffering from Seasonal Affective Disorder (SAD) and the turkey's going to be two hours late because there's a power cut. Oh dear!

— The Reality —

Well, obviously it all depends where you go. Moving from, say, Southampton to Brittany isn't going to achieve anything very much. Moving from Aberdeen to Malaga, on the other hand, is a massive change.

But the fact remains that the *perfect* climate is hard to come by. There are things called seasons which mean that while the weather might be perfect for, say, three months, there are nine months when it isn't. Too hot, too cold, too windy, too dry, too humid. And if you move to places where the temperature varies very little (the Caribbean) then you get bored – every day the same.

The real problem with seasons, though, is something else. Expats tend to do their exploring when the weather is at its most ideal and end up with a distorted impression. The best advice is to do the opposite – look around when the weather is at its *worst*.

Visit the northern Costa Brava in, say, June and you may pronounce the climate wonderful. But regularly in winter (and even occasionally in summer) there's something called the *tramuntana*. It's a wind from the mountains that spills down with incredible violence. For some reason, perhaps connected with global warming, it has lost some of its ferocity in recent years. But it can blow for days on end. People have actually been driven mad by it. The Catalans have a special word for this. They call it *atramuntanat* – driven crazy by the *tramuntana*.

OK, so you've seen your chosen destination in winter and you still like it. But what about high summer? Can you really cope with the heat? It all sounds very nice when you're freezing cold in Britain but

Enjoying a better climate

whoever said you can never have too much of a good thing never experienced the heat in, for example, Extremadura. The very words say it all. *Extrema* (from *extremadamente*) meaning extremely. *Dura* meaning hard. Can you imagine living in a place called extremely hard? You probably weren't thinking of going there anyway, but it's that part of southern Spain up against the Portuguese border including the towns of Badajoz and Cáceres. The temperatures there can approach 50°C (that's 122° Fahrenheit).

Everywhere in the Mediterranean summer temperatures can exceed 40°C and global warming is making the whole situation worse. In Catalonia in 2003 there were more consecutive days that exceeded 35°C than at any time since records began. It's one thing when you're lying on the beach, quite another when you have to work.

Where we live now (just inland of the Costa Brava) we start taking the odd siesta from around the middle of June. By July they're a frequent occurrence. And by the beginning of August they're unavoidable. When the temperature heads towards 40°C you simply pass out. Even so, siestas take some getting used to. Some people adjust to them straight away. Others wake up with a headache, feeling so groggy they can't think straight. We call it siesta skull.

One way of mitigating the problem is 'coastal influence'. By the sea you're virtually guaranteed offshore and onshore breezes and temperatures a few degrees lower than the interior. Maybe the effect will extend a kilometre inland, maybe more. It all depends. The problem is that that strip along the coast is going to be the most expensive (and crowded) real estate in the entire area. To be on the first rank (i.e. nothing between you and the beach) you'll pay maybe four times the price of a similar property inland. A little further back with a sea view maybe double. You might be better off buying inland and investing in air conditioning and a swimming pool.

If you don't like, or can't afford, air conditioning then, at the very least, buy a traditional property. They have thick stone walls for insulation, small windows to eliminate glare and heat, and vaults below ground level, to which people used to move their beds in summer.

Then there's the whole debate about skin cancer. Many experts say you shouldn't expose your skin to the sun at all. We think that's far too extreme and we're backed up by new research which shows that, by the end of winter, Britons are deficient in vitamin D from not having enough sunshine. We like to get a tan going as early in the year as possible then top it up whenever we can – but always without redness and seldom spending more than an hour actually sunbathing. We think it's safer than lying all day in the sun for two weeks and going bright red. The paradox is that in July and August we don't sunbathe in the garden at all. Too hot. Too many flies. Only on the beach where we can sprint across the burning sand to cool off in the water.

The corollary of plenty of sunshine is lack of rainfall. Your garden turns yellow and dies. The tap water tastes horribly chlorinated or, in some places, so brackish that you have to drink bottled water. You're dying for a cold shower but, because of rationing, you can't have one till tomorrow.

And then, of course, there are the insects. They say there may be 800 million insects in an acre of British farmland but at least you don't *see* them. In Mediterranean countries you do. Except, that is, for the midges. You only know they've been past by the lumps on your

Enjoying a better climate

body. The horse flies you won't have any trouble spotting, especially the ones with the big green eyes. If a horse isn't handy as a meal you'll do instead. So keep a horse.

OK, even southern England may reach the 30s some of the time. What makes Spain or Portugal or Greece or southern Italy different is that the heat is relentless. In England, for example, the temperature goes down significantly at night. And you also get cool spells. In the Mediterranean you don't. And eventually, the unremitting heat begins to wear you down. We have friends who now actually go *back* to Britain for July/August to escape the heat.

You can't move. You can't think. You go for a swim and the water doesn't refresh you. It feels like a bath. You sleep from 2pm till 4pm and wake up feeling as if you have a hangover. You start eating dinner at 10pm and going to bed at 2am. And even then it's still too hot. The temperature in the *bedroom* is 30°C. You're so lethargic you begin to believe you have a terminal illness.

And then, one evening, sitting on your terrace in your T-shirt, you suddenly notice something peculiar about your skin. It's covered in tiny pimples. Are you ill? No. Actually, for the first time in weeks you're feeling rather good. And then you realise. It's called September. You're cold. For the first time in three months you're actually *cold*. And it's wonderful.

— Pros —

☼ If you suffer from SAD (Seasonal Affective Disorder) then moving somewhere with more sunshine in winter will almost certainly make you feel better.

Do viđenja Engleska

- ☼ The action of sunshine on the skin produces vitamin D – essential for the health of skin and bones and protective against some cancers.
- ☼ Sunbathing – within sensible limits – just makes you feel *good*.
- ☼ There are many more days in the year when you can enjoy outdoor activities.

– Cons –

- A 'perfect' climate is attractive to people other than you. The place will be crowded and property prices high.
- If you sunbathe you increase your risk of skin cancer.
- Unrelenting high temperatures are wearing. You may have been a dynamo back in Britain but in the Mediterranean at the end of July you could be a wet rag.
- You just don't have the energy for the tennis, golf, horse riding and hiking that you were planning.
- Long, hot summers pose problems of their own, including drought and fire risk.
- Global warming is a reality so the climate where you live now might in time turn out to be more agreeable than the traditional sunspots.

Enjoying a better climate

– KEY QUESTIONS –

- Do you know what the climate is like every month, not just in August?
- If sunlight is more important than temperature, have you considered the mountains (the Alps or the Pyrenees)?
- The summer heat will be tempered by coastal influences – but can you afford a property on the coast?
- Have you ever experienced the kind of relentless heat that you will get in Spain, Portugal, southern Italy or Greece? Are you sure you can stand it? Is your health up to it? (It has been estimated that the 2003 heat wave cost tens of thousands of lives.)
- Is your property designed for the heat? Does it have adequate insulation in the roof? Outside shutters? Air-conditioning?
- Is a water supply guaranteed year round?
- Is there a fire risk? If so, are there trees close to the house?

2

Experiencing a different way of life

— The Dream —

You tip water into your *oúzo* until it turns cloudy, take a slug, reach for the *mezédhes*, select a chunk of *okhtapódhi* (octopus), settle back and listen to the *rembétika* singer on the radio, your worry beads hanging casually from your left hand. It's 6pm and you've been up for just one hour following the customary afternoon nap. And to think that, back in London at the same time, you would have been struggling home on the Circle Line. Any moment Odysseas will arrive for your first business meeting of the afternoon. You'll probably play *tavli* (backgammon) to get to know one another better. He'll almost certainly try to provoke you with an audacious move or two. That will be his method of feeling you out. But you, of course, will remain calm and gracious. Maybe next month you'll clinch the deal. It doesn't do to rush things.

Experiencing a different way of life

– The Reality –

We've travelled quite a bit. Visited every country in Europe and lived in France and Spain for 15 years. We both agree that Greek people, Spanish people, French people, German people, Italian people – you name it – are essentially no different from British people. Not in any fundamental way at all. Not a bit. They don't eat children. They're not mad. They don't settle disagreements by butting heads. They don't marry several people at the same time (no more than the British, anyway).

If we're talking Europe – and especially the most popular parts of Europe – life isn't going to be *that* different. But, then, maybe you don't want it to be *that* different. Just a little different. Which is fine.

Unless, of course, you count things like: drinking brandy for breakfast (Spain); believing *la famiglia è sacra* and threatening to kill anybody who insults your mother (Italy); or painting your café in your political colours (Greece).

It's all too easy, in any event, to continue the 'British' way of life in a foreign country. We, the British, have been doing it for centuries (while criticising immigrants to Britain for not integrating). Where there are Brits in significant numbers there are shops selling Marmite and all the rest of it, and satellite dishes to bring you British radio and television. After living abroad for 15 years we *still* listen to John Humphrys every morning and debate the British news with far more vigour than we do the Spanish.

Foreign food is no longer different. True, you won't find fish and chips, except perhaps in one of those *costa* cafés advertising 'English breakfast' and you certainly won't find the sort of flat, warm beer that John Major goes all nostalgic about. But let's face it, the standard British diet already relies heavily on foreign influences. The most popular meal is now chicken tikka while exotica such as pizza, pasta, tapas and taramosalata have all become commonplace.

Clothing? Well, it's a long time since Italians went round in togas. Nowadays, the same chains and the same clothes are in high streets everywhere from Piraeus to Paris. As a generalisation, Continentals tend to be more casual and yet, at the same time, more elegant. They spend more money on fewer clothes. And, in the Mediterranean, they scorn looking like tourists – that is, funny hats, sunglasses, shorts, flip flops and acres of bright red skin. That sort of thing is reserved strictly for the beach.

Even the famous mañana syndrome is exaggerated. If a plumber in Britain doesn't turn up for an appointment he's 'overworked'. In Spain, he's 'lazy'. That's not fair.

So what really *is* different? The most obvious thing is language. That, more than anything else, reminds you you're in a foreign country. The advantage is you won't understand when people insult you. The disadvantage is that, unless you speak very well, you're automatically going to be an outsider. If you live on your own or with no other English speaker to talk to you'll notice the isolation all the more.

Actually, even if you do speak the language you'll still be an outsider. And if you want to change that and get involved in any sort of political process you'll straight away run into the charge of 'foreigners telling us what to do'. We once tried to get up a petition against the shooting of thrushes. Where we live men in camouflage gear blast

Experiencing a different way of life

them in their thousands three or four days a week from early October to early February. Bad mistake!

Speaking of political processes, the mayor in a Mediterranean country has far more power than the British variety. They're no mere totem. Mayors have real power – and are far more likely to wield it on behalf of all the people they grew up with than an outsider.

The mayor, by the way, might be a woman but in the Mediterranean that's a lot less likely than in Britain. There's the machismo factor to take into account. The Catalan husband of an English friend of ours threw lunch at her when she dared to put avocado in the salad. The traditional salad, you see, is just lettuce, tomatoes, onion and olives. So feminists beware! Your hackles will be raised. Most of all in non-touristic, rural Greece where you won't be welcome in the all-male *kafenía*. When you're out with a man, another man will probably insist on speaking to you via your companion ("Does she take sugar?"). That's something you may not happily dismiss as 'local colour'. In Thrace they even have a festival called the *Gynaecocratia* (8 January) where women are allowed to go to the cafés and the men stay in and do the chores – which just underlines how different it is the other 364 days. Feminists had better steer clear of southern Italy, too, especially Calabria, Basilicata, Sardinia and Sicily, where cat-calling is pretty much the way of life.

But remote Greece and southern Italy are very particular places. Generally, we were surprised at the reaction of people in rural Spain, Portugal, France and most of Italy to the arrival of, for example, homosexual couples, mixed race couples and long haired hippies. There *was* no reaction. The British pride themselves on tolerance. So do Continentals.

Farvel England

Pace of life? Yes, it does tend to be slower but moving from, say, London to a remote village in the Massif Central can give you an exaggerated idea of things. People rush about just as much in Paris and Barcelona and Athens. Round our way they refer to townies as *nerviosos* – always agitated. What really makes a difference in the Mediterranean is the siesta – and the further south you go the longer it gets. That, in turn, means that people work later, play later and go to bed later, firstly because they've had an hour's sleep already and secondly it's the only time you can feel cool. Nightlife begins outdoors, when everyone parades up and down looking at everyone else. When the British are changing into their pyjamas the Portuguese, Spanish, Italians and Greeks are slipping into their gladrags. So there's a lot less need to rush. But even this is changing with, firstly, air conditioning and, secondly, commercial pressures. Just a few years ago no shops in Figueres, our nearest town, stayed open at lunchtime. Now several clothes shops and all large supermarkets do.

If we were asked to nominate one thing that's really different we'd probably say humanity. We wouldn't suggest there's more of it in mainland Europe than in Britain but there's certainly more of it than in London. In London you're just a pair of shoulders for someone else to climb up on. Here we're human beings. That is different.

— Pros —

- Moving somewhere new is bound to be a stimulating experience.
- Where you were born was simply an accident beyond your control so it may well be that you're much better suited to a different place.
- A change is as good as a rest.

Experiencing a different way of life

– Cons –

- Well, actually, nowhere in Europe is *that* different any more.
- The differences that do exist may not be ones you care for.
- You can make your life different, if you choose, whilst remaining in the UK.
- Eccentricity is more tolerated in Britain than in many other parts of Europe.
- You'll always be an outsider (which, depending on you, might also be a 'pro').

– KEY QUESTIONS –

- How much difference do you really want? Choose your location accordingly.
- Are you really willing to change yourself – or do you just want to watch other people being different?
- Can you be philosophical about differences that don't suit you?

3

Life will somehow be better

— The Dream —

You'll have a nice house. Although, come to think of it, the house you have right now in Britain isn't so bad. You'll earn a decent living. But, to be truthful, you're doing pretty well already. The sun will be shining but, to be fair, recently British summers have been a lot sunnier than they used to be. You'll have nice friends who'll come for Sunday lunch on the terrace. But, then, you have good friends in the UK you'll miss quite a lot. Yes, the water will be warm, clear and blue but you can't say Brighton beach isn't good fun. No, it isn't necessarily anything as specific as that. It's just that when you close your eyes and imagine how it'll be you see that running-through-cornfields thing. Your partner is bounding towards you in slow motion, dressed all in white, face tanned, radiant and loving. No more marriage counselling! And the kids are turning somersaults. You've never seen them so carefree. As for you, you're grinning like the proverbial Cheshire cat. Or should that be *gato*? No more Prozac!

Life will somehow be better

— The Reality —

Hemingway had a good phrase for this: never confuse movement with action. In other words, blindly responding to the impulse to 'do something' doesn't necessarily produce a positive result. Going abroad *might* make your life better. Equally, it might make it worse. Let's not forget that in France, Spain, Portugal, Greece, Croatia – in fact every country in the world – there are unhappy people whose lives are full of hardships and who also dream of escaping to a new country. Possibly even to Britain. A Greek will be astonished by your belief that you can solve all your problems (such as paying the mortgage) simply by moving to Greece where people, believe it or not, do have problems of their own (such as paying the mortgage).

And yet, and yet… Many people find there is an intangible *something* about living abroad that really does make life more enjoyable. It isn't necessarily anything specific like the job, the money or the house. It's…it's…something in the air. For some people, the mere fact of being abroad already counts for a lot. Abroad is romantic, exotic, daring, different. Even if it isn't actually better in any way you can quantify, it *seems* better.

Of course, a lot of it has to do with the frisson of the new. It's the same lift you get from a love affair. You're head over heels for someone. And yet that same person has just been chucked by somebody else for being boring. In the same way, we know plenty of young local people who are weary of the area we've moved to and who can't wait to get away (maybe to the UK). What's fresh and exciting to us is banal to them. The question is, will the love affair last? Or will it be a short lived infatuation?

All kinds of things plainly *aren't* better in most places abroad. The

UK, after all, rates pretty highly in things like standard of living, education, employment opportunities, personal freedom and a social security system which ensures nobody starves or goes without essential medical care. And, plainly, the vast majority of Brits are happy in their own country and wouldn't dream of leaving (but then, everybody always thinks their own country is the best in the world so that doesn't prove anything).

Being analytical, the odds are stacked against you in a foreign country. You'll probably be living somewhere you can't speak the language very well, if at all. If life was difficult in Britain do you really expect it to be any easier when you can't talk to people? If the kids weren't doing well at school in Britain how do you expect them to cope with lessons in French or Spanish or Greek? Nor will you have your relatives close by for support. (Some people might find that an advantage.) And you'll be burdening yourself with all kinds of additional chores and bureaucratic twaddle – the new driving licence, the residence permit, the wealth tax and all the rest of it.

Essentially, you'll be an outsider in a strange country. How you respond to that depends on your personality. Some people like the sense of detachment. The feeling that you're neither responsible for whatever is going on in Britain, nor as a stranger in a foreign land, for the things that are going on in Greece, or Switzerland…or wherever you happen to be. You're free of guilt. Free of the need to take action. But what some welcome as freedom others fear as a sense of isolation. It all depends on you but, in our experience, women find it harder than men to cope with the loss of friends and family support. If a relationship is already strained, moving abroad tends to make the situation worse, not better.

Personally, we're biased. We've loved all the places we've lived abroad –

Life will somehow be better

and we could envisage living in plenty of others (but not back in the UK). And it's not anything to do with practical things such as the standard of living. There is a kind of magic that operates for some of us.

For example, we spent two years living in a barn that, had it been in a town, would have been condemned as unfit for human habitation. Yet to us the gas lights, the leaking tin roof and the boards that moved as we walked on them all seemed so romantic. We were far happier than we had been in the mews cottage in London. Maybe it has something to do with a loss of ambition. Of course, there are still Gonzalezes, Leblancs and Papadopouloses to keep up with but somehow they don't seem to matter as much as the wretched Joneses who always caused such jealousy. No, maybe it's not a loss of ambition so much as acquiring new and more meaningful ambitions. Once away from those Joneses you see life from a different perspective.

On the other hand, if you move to a 'little Britain' on a swish golf course or marina where fast cars and speedboats abound you may find the old pressure to conform and measure up even worse than in the UK.

Life certainly isn't going to be better if you're just going to recreate the old patterns. Moving abroad isn't just about finding a new place but also the freedom to discover your true self. Hope you like it.

— Pros —

- The UK is a pretty tiny place (just 242,000 sq km out of 148,000,000 sq km or 0.16 percent of the land surface of the Earth) which suggests that, statistically, you're far more likely to find what you want *outside* the UK than inside.

Tot ziens Engeland

- ☼ A change can be a good thing.
- ☼ If you need hot, sunny weather, clear blue sea, high mountains or wilderness you certainly aren't going to find them in the UK.
- ☼ When you've got the itch you just *have* to scratch it.

— Cons —

- ☂ If you're very 'British' you'll miss things back home.
- ☂ Changing where you live doesn't automatically change other aspects of your life for the better.
- ☂ If your problems are the sort that travel with you, a new country won't change anything.
- ☂ You might escape problems in the UK but there will be plenty more where you're going.
- ☂ A recent survey found the Icelandics to have the highest 'Happy Life Expectancy' followed by the Swedes and the Dutch, confounding those who believe sunshine is essential for happiness.

— KEY QUESTIONS —

- Why aren't you happy where you are in Britain? Will the same reasons still apply if you live abroad?
- Do you find new challenges stimulating or do they tend to make you anxious?
- Would you feel guilty about 'running away' or do you think it's a sensible survival strategy?
- Is everybody (spouse/children) as optimistic about 'abroad' as you are? If not, any relationship problems are likely to get worse rather than better.

A less stressful pace of life

— The Dream —

You're driving through the village when you spot someone you know coming the opposite way. You wind down your window, wave and stop. Soon you're deep in conversation about the price of apples, two cars side by side, completely blocking the road. After a few minutes another car appears. It's Paco. You make a signal that you'll pull out of the way. But he's already getting out and strolling up to join you. "What do you think of the wine this year?" Five minutes later there are half a dozen cars pulled up and you're all enjoying a joke together. Nobody is in too much of a hurry to ignore the truly important things in life.

Adiaua Anglio

— The Reality —

Yes, the reality can be like that. It can. Many times we've stopped in the village to talk to someone and held the traffic up for a minute or so. Nobody minds. It's normal. Equally we've got used to waiting for other people to have a chat. On one occasion – in France – a farmer was delivering hay for our ponies and blocked the road for 20 minutes. Nobody complained. But it's not the sort of thing you'd do in Rome or Barcelona.

It has much more to do with country life, of course, than with life abroad. It also has to do with what we call the 'inverse earnings rule'. In other words, wealthy people on large salaries (who could therefore easily afford to make time for life's little pleasantries) are invariably brusque. While poor people (who theoretically should be desperate not to have their earnings reduced) are those most inclined to stop to pass the time of day. These things apply everywhere.

So is there really a Continental component? Is there really any evidence that life is less stressful in some other European countries? Well, actually, yes there is. The EU periodically carries out Labour Force Surveys which suggest that stress, depression and anxiety associated with work are at crisis level in the UK when compared with the European average. In the most recent survey it accounted for 30.5 percent of all work related health problems for men and a staggering 36.5 percent for women. If you want to avoid stress at work, Spain seems to be your best bet. There only 7.3 percent of work related health problems are caused by stress for men and 8.7 percent for women. In southern Europe, Greece would be your next choice, followed by Italy, followed by Portugal. But this is not a case

A less stressful pace of life

of a north-south divide. Stress seems to be less of a problem *everywhere* in Europe than it is in the UK.

Hours worked certainly have something to do with it. The British put in almost 45 hours a week (according to Eurostat, the EU's statistics service) and 4 million slave more than 50 hours (50 percent more people than in 1984). But if working hours alone are the problem, there's no point going to Greece (44.5 hours), Portugal (43.1 hours) or Spain (42.3 hours), which are the next three worst places. Better to choose France (41 hours) or Denmark (40 hours). Best bet with sunshine is Italy at 40.6 hours.

But, really, it isn't so much the number of hours as the pressure. A recent TUC survey found that 62 percent of respondents said overwork was causing stress, while in the finance and insurance sector this was as high as 91 percent.

The Mediterranean countries are notorious for a mañana attitude, which covers a lot more than the timing of appointments. A laid back Italian understands that you shouldn't drive the wrong way down a one way street when cars are coming – he just doesn't understand why you shouldn't do it if the road is empty. No Greek would dream of driving through a red light when there's traffic – but supposing there's no traffic? And every Spanish kid on a motorcycle understands that he has to wear a crash helmet. And he does. On his arm. By the way, these youngsters also take a delight in removing the silencers (or removing the baffles from inside the silencers) so as to make as much noise as possible. Very relaxing!

But at least some of this mañana stuff is in the eye of the beholder. Plenty of British plumbers will also tell you 'tomorrow' whilst actually meaning 'next week' or 'next month'.

So let's not exaggerate. When something *has* to be done urgently, people will respond. (The thing is, what you think of as urgent may not seem very urgent to them.) And many people in country areas work extremely hard indeed, from first light until dusk. Much harder, in many cases, than people in towns. One of the hardest working men we've ever come across owns the garage in a nearby village. Almost any time of day, any day of the week, including Sundays, he can be found lying under someone's car, jeep, tractor or harvesting machine, covered in oil. Nor will you see much of the 'slower pace of life' if you have the misfortune to work in, say, the kitchen of a seafront café. No, it's really that the countryside induces a more philosophical approach to life. Things are linked to natural cycles and the weather and can't be *forced*. No matter how dynamic you are, you can't harvest a crop until it's ready.

So you've decided to move abroad. Very sensibly you've decided on a rural retreat far from cities and far from tourists. But there's just one problem. You see, according to experts, anything that causes a change in your life actually *causes* stress. So it's Catch 22: whatever you do to reduce stress actually *introduces a new stress*.

The experts say that the death of a spouse is the most stressful event in anybody's life. If we put that at 100 on the stressometer, then leaving your job is about 35, a change to your financial circumstances is also 35, a change in your living conditions is 20, in your personal habits 20 and in the frequency of family get togethers 10. That's already 120 you're going to incur before factoring in life abroad. Oh, by the way, a hot climate is also stress.

So *take it easy*. If you can't slow down you probably won't fit in and your antics won't go unnoticed nor uncriticised. In fact, you'll probably be the target for a lot of humour. People from towns tend to

A less stressful pace of life

have the feeling they don't exist or have any significance if they're not rushing somewhere. A lot of expats bring their stressed out attitudes with them. It takes some a year or even two before they slow to the rhythm of the locals.

— Pros —

- UK working hours are the longest in Europe and stress related illness at work is the highest in Europe. Moving abroad (though not the USA) is almost guaranteed to be better for your physical and mental health.
- Stress may be responsible for a wide range of illnesses including hypertension, heart disease, impaired immune system (leading to viral disorders, colds, herpes and many other problems), depression, alcoholism and drug abuse.
- If stress at work is your problem, Spain is the place to go — followed by Greece, Italy and Portugal.

— Cons —

- Moving abroad will itself cause stress.
- Stress is only bad for you when you can't cope with it. Lots of people thrive on stress and consider it essential to their performance. You may find you become less dynamic and less creative without it. People are like violin strings. Too much stress and they snap. Too little and they don't resonate as they should.
- When you want something done urgently you may be frustrated by the lack of stress in other people — the famous mañana syndrome.
- A foreign country introduces new sources of stress — coping with the language, wrestling with bureaucracy and being isolated from family and friends.

Adiaua Anglio

☂ Rather than go abroad you might reduce stress through yoga or meditation, a change of job or a move to the countryside.

> — KEY QUESTIONS —
>
> - Are you suffering from stress? Why? Would a move abroad really change anything?
> - Yes, you'd like to take life a bit slower yourself, but are you also willing for *other* people to take life more slowly?
> - Are you sure a move to the British countryside wouldn't suit you better than going abroad?

5

A healthier lifestyle

— The Dream —

You've just come back from your early morning run around the lake. The air is so invigorating and clean and it's hard to remember the last time rain stopped you going. Now you settle down to your breakfast of low fat goat's cheese from the farm at the end of the lane. You'll work in your study till 1pm, then it will be lunch of grilled vegetables sprinkled with organic olive oil. How wonderful not to have to commute to work any more. This afternoon you'll have a go at repairing the dry stone wall. It's hard, but your partner needn't think you'll be a pushover at tennis afterwards. Tonight you'll have trout washed down by some of that fruity local wine. You're looking forward to the weekend — a barbecue on the beach and swimming races with the kids.

— The Reality —

It's curious that British people should think life is healthier abroad, because people in most other European countries think of themselves as being relatively unhealthy.

Figures from Eurostat (the European statistics agency) show that 11.5 percent of EU citizens[3] over 16 consider their health to be bad or very bad, compared with 9.5 percent for Brits. People in Greece and France assess their health similarly to people in the UK, but the Italians are slightly more pessimistic and the Portuguese enormously so – which may explain their mournful *fado* music. For those aged 65 and over the picture is more dramatic. In the UK 15.7 percent in this age group think their health is bad or very bad, compared with *more than half* of the Portuguese. In fact, only Irish, Belgian and Dutch pensioners are more optimistic about their health than British pensioners.

All right. These are highly subjective views. Believing your health is good or bad doesn't mean it is. What, then, are the facts? What about things like air and water pollution, for example?

The European Pollutant Emission Register (EPER) which records the release of pollutants into the air and water reveals that north east Spain, northern France and northern Italy are as worrying as the more industrialised parts of Britain. And in 2004 the European Commission targeted nine countries for legal action over air pollution, including Spain, Italy, Greece and Portugal, but *excluding* Britain (and France).

So Britain may not be so bad, after all.

[3] The 15 EU countries prior to 2004

A healthier lifestyle

What about nutrition?

A big claim for better health is the famous Mediterranean diet, involving plenty of olive oil, garlic, vegetables – especially tomatoes – and fruits. Most experts agree on its benefits. Research shows that garlic and olive oil are two of the most potent 'medicinal foods' with the ability to fight infection, reduce the risk of cancer, thin the blood and lower both cholesterol and blood pressure. And there's also good evidence that tomatoes reduce the risk of certain cancers. So far so good.

In the UK, circulatory diseases including heart attacks are the commonest cause of death by illness. By contrast, the rate in France and Spain is much lower, which looks like support for the Mediterranean diet. Yet the rate in Greece is just as bad as in Britain, Italy is quite high and Portugal is only marginally better. Nor is the Mediterranean any more proof against cancer than the North Sea.

In fact, other aspects of the Mediterranean diet are less encouraging. Vegetarianism and veganism are far less popular in the Mediterranean area than in the more 'puritanical' north where self denial is a virtue. Olive oil there may be but it comes served with huge quantities of meat and fish. We all now know the dangers of excessive meat consumption but surely fish is healthy? Well, yes, in principle it is. It's just that nowadays it's full of dangerous pollutants. The situation is so worrying that the UK Food Standards Agency (FSA) issued new guidelines in 2004 of 140 grams of oily fish a week for males and women past child bearing age, and a maximum of two portions a week for other women. Particularly worrying are toxins such as methylmercury in large predatory fish, and dioxins and PCBs in all fish (thankfully 70 percent down in the environment in last 10 years). Oh, and Mediterranean people tend to counter any beneficial effects of the Mediterranean diet with huge quantities of cheap tobacco.

The obvious point, though, is that there's no need to go to the Med to enjoy the benefits of the Mediterranean diet. Everything you need is in the local British supermarket. So that really isn't an argument.

The next thing is the slower pace of life. We'll leave that aside as it's dealt with in the previous chapter, except to say that, yes, on average, people are less stressed (see *A Less Stressful Pace Of Life*).

Another ingredient is getting out of doors more often and taking exercise. It's a fact that you can lose a pound of body weight by burning 3,500 calories. And being overweight is connected with all kinds of health problems. A study of elderly men in Honolulu showed that those who walked more than one and a half miles a day had half the rate of heart disease of those who walked a quarter of a mile or less. Case proven. But will you *really* take more exercise? We know plenty of expats whose lifestyles revolve around alcohol and the next restaurant. In summer, it's as much as many people can do to walk from their air conditioned home to their air conditioned car, let alone exert themselves in any way. We certainly find we exercise far less in the summer than the rest of the year. About the only place you feel vigorous is in the sea, but the beach means increased risk of skin cancer. Between 1995 and 2000 the number of Brits diagnosed with melanoma increased by 24 percent. You have to take it seriously – it kills 1,600 Brits a year when the melanoma spreads to other parts of the body.

Regular health checks are seen by many as a preventive. Nowadays they're a growing feature of the National Health. But they're not easily available in most Mediterranean destinations. If you pay

A healthier lifestyle

Spanish social security (*Seguridad Social*), for example, you'll get free or subsidised medical and dental treatment on the same basis as Spanish people, but free check-ups are few and far between. You're going to have to pay for most of them – and for most dental work, too.

Car accidents are an important cause of early death. Britain is one of the safest countries in the world when it comes to traffic accidents. According to Eurostat, you're roughly four times more likely to be killed in a transport accident in Greece than in the UK. A man is three times as likely to die that way in Portugal as in the UK (and a woman more than twice as likely). Spain isn't much better. And the risk is twice as high in France and Italy.

The bottom line, of course, is life expectancy. Quite honestly, there really isn't much in it between Britain and the Mediterranean countries – a couple of years at most. If you're a man you'll do far better changing your sex than your country. You could add three or four years that way.

— Pros —

- The Mediterranean diet has proven health benefits.
- The more relaxed lifestyle in much of southern Europe must be good for you.
- The climate in southern Europe is conducive to lots of healthy fresh air and outdoor activity.

— Cons —

- The very act of moving abroad is stressful and, therefore, unhealthy (see *A Less Stressful Pace Of Life*).

Näkemiin Englanti

- You can enjoy the Mediterranean diet just as much in the UK as in the Mediterranean.
- A lot of expat social life is fuelled by regular, large quantities of inexpensive alcohol. Tobacco is cheap, too.
- Parts of mainland Europe have far worse pollution than the UK.
- Traffic accidents are more common in Mediterranean countries than they are in Britain.
- If you spend a lot of time in the healthy outdoors you may increase your risk of skin cancer.

– KEY QUESTIONS –

- Are you *really* going to change your eating habits, anyway?
- Will you *really* exercise more, just because the sun is shining?
- What sort of health cover have you got? If you're working in other EU countries you'll generally enjoy the same health benefits as citizens of that country (which may not be as comprehensive as the NHS) but if you're just enjoying yourself (or in the 'black' economy) you won't. If necessary, can you afford private health cover?
- Do you have a known risk of melanoma? Can you cope with heat?
- Will you be able to resist cheap booze and fags?
- Are you sure the place you're moving to actually *is* healthier? Check things like pollution and standards of preventive health care.

6

A better place to bring up children

— The Dream —

Eight year old John switches effortlessly into Spanish whilst he discusses with his friends where they'll go. They decide to take their snorkelling gear and head for the beach. You're not worried because he's become a very strong swimmer since you moved to the Mediterranean, his lean sun-tanned body darting like a fish through the limpid waters. It's good to see how strong and healthy he's become. As for 13 year old Melanie, she's off on the train to Girona with her school pals. They're going to paint watercolours of the old houses overhanging the Rio Oñar. It's wonderful that she has such nice friends. So well brought up. So polite. Those traditional values that have almost disappeared in Britain.

– The Reality –

It would be ludicrous to suggest that every place abroad is better for children than any place in Britain. But a lot of parents have concluded that the best places abroad are better than most places in Britain.

However, the experiences of parents who moved with young children are sharply different from those who moved with older children. The message seems to be: *don't delay*. The younger they make the move the better. Every day that passes, their ability to pick up a foreign language goes down. The ideal age seems to be anything under six or seven. Ten is the watershed.

We have British friends who moved to Spain and stoically put their two girls (aged four and seven) into the Catalan speaking local primary school. The first day everybody was in tears (the children and the parents). But by the end of one month of 'tough love' the children were already speaking enough Catalan to be invited to friends' houses and within three months they were almost fluent. (Not so the parents who still struggle after two years.)

There's a difference between assimilating the language and learning it. Learning is a chore and calls for enormous motivation. Young children do pick up foreign languages very easily without formal lessons, provided they're surrounded by people speaking it all day. But if you go to a British enclave where there are British children to play with and if, when they get home, everybody watches British TV by satellite, they won't learn. These same two girls were the first British children in their school. Now, two years later, there are 10. That's how fast the whole living abroad thing is taking off. Great,

A better place to bring up children

you say. My children will fit in so much more easily. Yes, but they'll only be fitting in with the other British children, not the local children.

The whole thing becomes so much harder when your children are older. It's going to take them longer to learn the language and their education is going to be set back quite significantly. For them it makes sense to learn the language *before* going.

Expat friends with children tell us Spain provides the kind of childhood they themselves enjoyed in the 1960s – the freedom to stroll in the countryside or go to the beach without fear of being attacked. The question of safety, however, is very much a matter of perception. It isn't for nothing the *Costa del Sol* is known as the *Costa del Crime* (largely because of the activities of non-Spanish gangs). The drug problem is everywhere and the attitude is far more relaxed in many European countries than in Britain – especially Spain, Switzerland and the Netherlands. Cannabis for personal consumption has long been tolerated in Spain, for example. You'll see cannabis plants in the gardens and terraces of plenty of your friends. If you're horrified at the idea of your children coming into contact with the cannabis culture then Spain isn't for you. But if you take the view that cannabis is more on a par with alcohol – something to be used occasionally and in moderation – you'll be more in tune with youth culture there.

If all this sounds worrying then France is a better bet for you, with its far less tolerant approach. But even there it's estimated that, despite the French police uprooting over 40,000 plants a year (compared with 1,500 a decade ago) three million people, mostly youngsters, still smoke cannabis regularly.

Auf Wiedersehen England

Another worry for British parents is the late night. In Britain you might be freaking out if your daughter wasn't back home by 11pm. In Spain, Italy and the more touristic parts of Greece she won't even be going out until 11pm. The fact is that nobody goes to a disco before midnight. Looking on the bright side, you don't have to go out at 1am to collect them. You can get a full night's sleep and pick them up in time for breakfast. And that's not a joke. That's just how it is.

Then there are motorbikes. In Britain it's not so difficult to bribe a child to wait for a car. In some European countries, on the other hand, you can't drive a car till you're 18 but you can drive a low powered motorbike at14. That four year gap makes it a whole lot harder. Add in a rate of fatal road accidents that, in most cases, is far higher than Britain's and you have something else to worry about. In Greece the rate is five times higher, in Spain three times higher, in France double and in Italy almost double. And motorbikes are the most dangerous of all.

Maybe your children will be different. Maybe they won't want to go to discos. Maybe they're very clear about saying 'No' to drugs. Maybe they won't be attracted to motorbikes. After all, none of this is obligatory. It's just that there's a lot of it around.

If you're not just moving abroad but also moving to a very different environment this could pose additional adjustment problems. For example, moving from a large British city to the French countryside. Children tend to want very different things from their parents. They need friends and they need things to do. Listening to the peace and quiet is unlikely to appeal. Finding the place to suit such diverse needs is not going to be easy.

A better place to bring up children

Finally, what will your children do when they grow up? The sort of place you dream of moving to is probably not the best place for them to start a career. If you're in the countryside or a resort they'll almost certainly have to move if they want a high flying job.

— Pros —

- Your children will speak at least two languages fluently (English plus the language of the country you're going to).
- Your children will grow up with a less insular, more international outlook.
- Your children will benefit from everything your adopted home has to offer – the climate, the beach, the mountains or whatever.

— Cons —

- If your children are nearing the end of primary schooling or older the move is going to be a terrific wrench.
- Children find it far more traumatic than adults to leave close friends behind.
- Older children will be set back in their education.
- Unless you're bringing your own parents with you you'll be cutting yourselves off from family support and babysitting services.
- Very long summer holidays tend to be the rule in the Mediterranean (almost three months in Spain) which can make parents' lives very difficult.
- Drug problems are no different from the UK.
- Traffic accidents are more prevalent than in the UK.

Auf Wiedersehen England

— KEY QUESTIONS —

- Do the children have very close friends they'll miss?
- Are they already too old to learn a new language easily (i.e. over10)?
- Is the new lifestyle going to be very different from what they're used to or will it be something they'll readily adapt to?
- Is the education system compatible with what they've been used to?
- Do you want an international school where lessons are taught in English or do you think the local school is preferable?
- Where do you envisage the children beginning their careers, in your adopted country or in Britain?

7

Life will be cheaper

— The Dream —

A little self-satisfied smile plays at the corners of your mouth. It was a smart move. You earn money in Britain from consultancy work and some well chosen investments but live in Spain where costs are relatively low. You get so much more for your money. The house for a start. You could never have afforded anything like this in Britain. Then, taxation is so much lower. Even the road fund licence. Food is cheaper. Switching to diesel — significantly less than petrol — was another smart move. The cost of help around the house and garden is affordable — you could never have had a gardener in Britain. Basically, your financial problems have all been solved. It's as if you've become, at a stroke, much richer. So why not celebrate with some *cava* — the local 'champagne'? After all, it only costs about £1 a bottle.

— The Reality —

So what is the truth about the cost of living in Britain, compared with other countries? Statistics can come to our aid here.

Well, London is notorious for being expensive, regularly in the top 10 most costly cities in the world and, amongst European cities, regularly in the top five. Even Paris is usually outside the top 20 while Rome isn't even in the top 40. So if you live in London now almost anywhere you move is bound to be cheaper. But London isn't Britain. In fact, recent EU figures suggest the cost of living in the UK is actually quite low compared with other European countries and markedly lower than the Scandinavian countries. The bottom line is that the only EU countries where life is *significantly* cheaper are Poland, Estonia, Latvia and Slovakia.

Not convinced?

Another way of getting at the truth is to see how households spend their money. According to Eurostat (the EU statistical agency), people in the UK spend just fractionally above the European average on housing, water, electricity and other fuel. Move to Portugal or Greece and you'll definitely spend less on these items. But the more telling statistic is that when it comes to what's *left over* for recreation, hotels and restaurants, people in the UK had more of their income to spend than anybody else in Europe, including the Germans. The main reason is that Brits spend proportionately less on food than most other Europeans.

Still not convinced?

OK, let's take a look at household disposable income. The calcula-

Life will be cheaper

tions are quite complicated because of the need to convert to a common 'purchasing power' and adjust for different household size. But, basically, the most recent figures show that Brits have far more disposable income than the EU average and half as much again as people in Portugal and Greece (despite the lower cost of services there), a third more than people in Spain and a quarter more than those in Italy.

Of course, the situation is always changing and official statistics tend to lag behind. But the whole idea of EU membership is that the standard of living in poorer countries should be fast tracked up to the level of the richer countries. Which inevitably means the cost of living will be going up, too. (Something people in countries like Spain, Portugal and Greece are always complaining about.) So the situation for Brits moving to 'low cost' European countries is likely to get worse, not better.

Bear in mind, too, that it's notoriously difficult to make meaningful comparisons for individuals because everyone's spending patterns are different. It's irrelevant that alcohol and tobacco are cheap in Spain if you don't drink or smoke.

One thing's for sure, moving abroad is going to introduce a whole new category of expenditure that you didn't have in the UK. Number one is the cost of going back to Britain for business or personal reasons. A few lucky people may not need to but most of us have to make several trips a year. No-frills airlines have made a considerable difference here, but if you're not served by a low cost carrier then this could be pretty painful. Then there's the phone bill. You're going to be making a lot more international calls than you used to.

Viszontlátásra Anglia

The good news is that, just as no-frills airlines have revolutionised air travel, so budget telephone companies and the internet have dramatically cut the cost of communications. When we first moved abroad 15 years ago our telephone bill was horrifying. Likewise the cost of postage. Now we spend only a third of what we did on communications. There aren't many things you can say that about. Whatever else you do, make sure you sign up with a budget telephone service and if you're not yet 'computer literate' then learn fast. (For the benefit of the truly Luddite we'd like to point out that you can even use a webcam to see the folks back home and let them see you.)

While we're on the subject of technology, you can also use the internet to buy a whole range of consumer durables at the lowest prices in the world. (But don't forget that the cost of post and packaging – and insurance – can add quite a lot to the final bill.) In that way, it doesn't matter *where* you live or how many hundreds of kilometres you are from the nearest superstore. What does still count, though, is food shopping. If you've moved to the countryside you may be some way from a supermarket. Shopping in the village store is bound to be expensive. You'll also find things unusually expensive in tourist resorts. Ski resorts are the worst. Cut off from the world below, prices might be anything from 20 percent to 100 percent higher than in the valley towns.

Then there's yet another category of expenditure you probably haven't even thought of: professional advice. Things that you used to handle on your own in Britain may prove – with language complications – insurmountable in some foreign countries. In Spain, even the Spanish employ *gestors* to deal with bureaucratic nightmares for them. Not only is the paperwork complicated but, in

Life will be cheaper

addition, you can spend your entire life queuing up. As a foreigner you stand even less chance of sorting things out (and probably have better things to do) so factor in professional help as a necessary extra expense. And include something for professional language tuition, while you're at it. Young children just soak up new languages but for adults it's a long and painful business.

Tax? As somebody already said, it's one of only two sure things in life along with death. Millions of British people are convinced they're the most hard done by in the world and that living abroad is the only solution. But, believe us, you aren't going to get away with tax that easily. Yes, on the face of it, some taxes are lower than in Britain – but other taxes are higher. In Spain there's a wealth tax, for example. You don't get that in Blighty. It's on a sliding scale ranging from 0.2 percent for assets of around £100,000 up to 2.5 percent. You'd have to be pretty rich to pay the top rate but, remember, wealth doesn't just mean your house or shares; it also covers cars, boats, cash and even jewellery. France has a wealth tax, too, though you've got to be pretty rich to pay it.

The real test is what the men in suits call 'total tax pressure' – the slice of the overall cake that goes to the government. In Britain it's under 40 percent (obviously it varies from year to year). Go to Portugal, Spain or Greece and the government's take is only around a third, but in France and Italy it's even higher than in Britain. Instead of complaining spare a thought for the Swedes and the Danes – the government takes about half their money. Just in case you're planning something crafty, remember what happened in Portugal. Some expats there thought it would be a good tax wheeze to put their homes in the names of offshore companies. And it was – until the Portuguese authorities imposed a special 5 percent tax

Viszontlátásra Anglia

on them. Remember, taxes and death are unavoidable. But if taxation is really an issue try Mexico – the government's take there is under 20 percent.

What it really comes down to then is this. If you've already made your pile, or your earnings come from the UK, you could be better off in countries like Portugal and Greece and even Spain and Italy. If you've got a house to sell in the South East that you've owned for 20 years you're going to be able to liberate plenty of capital for the farmhouse in the Massif Central or Thessaly (or, come to that, Sutherland). But if you're expecting to make your living abroad you could end up *worse* off. If you're earning, say, £30,000 a year in Britain now you might find you'll be on £20,000 around the Mediterranean.

— Pros —

- In some parts of Europe, the cost of living *is* cheaper than in the UK.
- Items that may be considerably cheaper, depending where you're going in Europe, include housing, petrol/diesel, alcohol/tobacco, labour.

— Cons —

- If you're earning your living in the country you're going to, you'll probably earn less than in the UK.
- In some popular destinations – especially tourist resorts – the cost of living is likely to be *higher* than the UK average.
- Living abroad may save some costs but introduce new ones – return trips to the UK, telephone calls, postage, professional advice.

Life will be cheaper

— KEY QUESTIONS —

- Where will your earnings come from? The UK or 'abroad'?
- What is the chance of Britain joining the euro? What impact is that likely to have on your financial situation?
- What is the tax situation in your dream country?
- How often will you want/need to return to the UK? How much will it cost to fly back when necessary?
- What is the cost of telephone calls to the UK? Are there budget operators?
- Yes, the cost of living in your chosen destination may be lower *on average* but how does it compare for the *specific* things you want?

Enjoying outdoor sports

— The Dream —

It's another beautiful day. Do you get your skis out and drive up to the nearest ski station, just under an hour away? Or do you slip down to the coast and hire a couple of sea kayaks? Or maybe amble over to the farm and see about a ride? It's hard to choose. Finally, you decide to go riding. Quite soon you're both in the saddle and heading along the little track by the stream. You cross at the ford and take the path that climbs up to the oak woods. Now it's lunchtime. You sit eating your picnic, the sun beating down. You rub some sun screen onto your faces and bare arms. And yet it's only March. Perfect! The only problem is that tomorrow you're going to face the same agonising decisions all over again.

Enjoying outdoor sports

— The Reality —

There's no denying that in mainland Europe there's an awful lot more of the Great Outdoors than there is in Britain. With an average of 250 people on every square kilometre of the UK there isn't an awful lot of space left over for things like skiing, hiking or riding. In Spain and Greece the population density is only one third the UK figure, in France two fifths and in Portugal less than half. That's a lot more room to work up a sweat in.

We live a little inland from the Mediterranean coast with mountains rising up behind. The things that we do regularly, within a manageable drive, include swimming, diving, sailing, hiking, riding, skiing and snowboarding. Within the area, we've also had a go at sea kayaking, windsurfing, canyoning, caving, parascending and dog mushing. And that's only a fraction of the things we could do. We're neither athletic nor daring and in Britain we hardly did any of these things. We just didn't feel like it. Here we do.

So we've got to admit to prejudice here. We enjoy the Mediterranean's Great Outdoors and we found it difficult to come up with any 'cons'. About the worst thing we can think to say about outdoor sports in mainland Europe is that you won't find it easy to play cricket. Nor croquet nor crown green bowling. Dwyle flonking isn't very popular, either.

After a lot of effort, then, here are some of the ways in which the more popular outdoor activities are at a disadvantage in the Mediterranean region compared with the UK:

Watersports. 'Either too much wind or none at all!' That's something you'll often hear from the mouths of Mediterranean yachtsmen and

Arrivederci Inghilterra

windsurfers and there's a modicum of truth in it. But only a modicum. More serious for traditional (i.e. wooden) boats is the teredo (a wood eating parasite) which thrives in warmer waters and can reduce planking to wafer biscuits within a few weeks. But the biggest problem of all is the popularity of the Med in summer.

If like us you want to be 'at one' with the sea and not just use it as a sort of watery motorway for roaring up and down on, you'll get fed up with the noise of speedboats, the wake that spills your wine when you're at anchor and, above all, those annoying jet ski things which ruin the tranquillity. Not to mention the fact that the water in your favourite bay is covered with a film of oil and the little beach littered with washed up beer cans, bottles and plastic bags. Every man and his dog takes to the Med and, quite frankly, the dogs would often make a better job of being in charge. The Med looks so easy that nobody bothers to learn things like the effects of wind or tidal currents or how to set an anchor properly, with sometimes disastrous results.

Our answer to both teredos and lunatics is to lay the boat up in mid-summer, do all the painting and varnishing, and put it back in the water in the middle of September. You'll fry any teredos in the wood, save a fortune in marina charges and be back in the water as soon as the lunatics have gone. And, let's face it, the Solent isn't exactly undiscovered, either. So on balance we prefer to do our boating where a birthday suit is more general than a suit of oilskins.

Score UK 0 : Mainland Europe 1

Golf. Complaints include high green fees (especially the Costa del Sol), long advance booking, slow rounds, too many other golfers, too much heat in summer, too many olive trees in the way and too

Enjoying outdoor sports

many 19th hole hangovers. In general, British golfers miss the heather, the sheep and the subtlety of UK courses. So the UK is the winner.

Running score UK 1: Mainland Europe 1

Riding. Mediterranean summers are misery for horses and riders alike. It's far too hot between about 9am and 9pm. Streams are dried up and grass burnt yellow. And there are irritating flies everywhere, from tiny ones which get in the horses' ears to huge green eyed monsters which suck blood by the syringe full. None of this is conducive to enjoyable hacking. But once again there is a solution: just ride the other 10 months of the year. From our house we have tracks and paths leading off in every direction and in some areas we can just canter off along the open mountainsides. That's a freedom it's very hard to find in most of Britain. Not only that, but the climate means horses can live out of doors, at a considerable saving.

Running score UK 1 : Mainland Europe 2

Wintersports. We won't say too much about snowsports here because they're dealt with under *Being Near Ski Slopes*. The only downside we can think of is that global warming will eventually wreck wintersports in southern Europe. But, even so, Britain won't get any more alluring, mainly because it hasn't got any decent mountains. After all Ben Nevis, the highest mountain in the UK, is a mere 1,343 metres. Our kitchen used to be higher than that (1,478 metres to be precise). Nobody can really argue this one. The Alps provide the best on-piste skiing in the world and our local stations in the Pyrenees aren't far behind.

Running score UK 1 : Mainland Europe 3

Arrivederci Inghilterra

Wildlife. Theoretically, there's far more wildlife to see in the Mediterranean outdoors than in Britain. But that is only theory. Due to Mediterranean man's passion for shooting things, a huge amount of wildlife is either close to extinction or cowering in the most inaccessible places. You'll probably see more in a Sussex back garden. On a trek along the Pyrenees, for example, you won't any longer see ibex (hunted to extinction), nor wolves, nor lynx, nor bear (hunted almost to extinction). Despite living in a semi-wilderness in Spain we seldom see foxes, badgers, squirrels, deer, wild boar or even rabbits. That's all thanks to hunting.

Running score UK 2 : Mainland Europe 4

– Pros –

- In mainland Europe you have the choice of the world's finest combination of landscape and climate for whatever you want to do.
- Things that are really demanding in Britain due to the weather and tidal currents are often much easier in other parts of Europe (no tides in the Mediterranean, for example).

– Cons –

There aren't any really, but…
- When it comes to messing around in boats, the Mediterranean is far tougher on wood than the UK. And it's not all seas like a mirror – violent storms can blow up with little warning.
- The popularity of some parts of Europe means they can be very crowded in the summer.
- Summers down south aren't conducive to any physical activity at all other than swimming.

Enjoying outdoor sports

– KEY QUESTIONS –

- Do you enjoy any outdoor sports now? If not, what makes you think you will if you move abroad?
- If getting out on the Med is your dream, do you want a motor boat or a sailing boat? (Listen, friend, you want a sailing boat – less noise, less pollution. Right?) What size of boat do you need – will you actually spend nights on board? Will you go cruising or will you just potter around locally? Where will you keep the boat? Marinas are expensive, especially in summer. Would you be better with a boat you can keep at home and transport to the beach (i.e. an inflatable, a sea kayak, a sailing dinghy or, anyway, something small enough to go on a trailer)?
- If having a horse is your dream, where will you keep it? Do you have enough land (in the Mediterranean you generally need about 2 hectares per horse unless you're going to rely on bought-in feed)? Who will look after the horse when you're not there? (There's a saying where we live that keeping animals is slavery – and you're the slave.)
- Can you actually afford the time and the money for the sports you aspire to? Activities like skiing, sailing, paragliding and riding are all pretty expensive.

Making a new start

— The Dream —

The lights are on in the garden. The sound system pumps out something smoochie. Your guests dance on the patio or gather in little groups to chat. It's wonderful to have all these friends. Even better that not a single one of them knew you two years ago. No one therefore knows your ex-wife or why she left you. Nobody knows that your business failed back in the UK and you almost went bankrupt. Nobody knows about the drinking problem and the breakdown. All of that is behind you, now. And look what you've accomplished in two years. A new home in Portugal. A new and successful business. The respect of the local community. Given your past, you never could have achieved any of that back in the UK.

Making a new start

— The Reality —

This whole subject of 'running away' for a new start is something of a favourite of ours. We're perfectly familiar with the old adage that you can't run away from yourself. But we have a sneaking suspicion it was written by a man in a suit who was afraid of what might happen if people discovered freedom. We tend to take the view that when you run away from something you're running *towards* something else, even if you don't know what it is. And that something else could be just right for you.

Flashback 25 years and we were both relatively urban types, working hard at our jobs in London, no strangers to wine bars and concerts and Bond Street shopping.

Now fast forward to today and we're both scruffy outdoor types with a boat, a cupboard full of gear for diving, hiking, skiing and snowboarding, a paddock out the back with five ponies and a saddlery with a couple of handsome Western rigs. Neither of us has worn any formal clothes for 15 years. You'll search the house in vain for a business suit.

Nobody who knew us then would have predicted it. Nor would we ourselves. And if we'd stayed at our desks in London none of it would ever have happened.

So, yes, we believe in new starts. Let's face it, the French Foreign Legion was built on the idea that you could run away and start over (though you'd have to be running away from something pretty awful to think the Foreign Legion an improvement). The British have quite a history of it, too. Byron famously said goodbye to 'perfidious Albion' and went in search of a new life in Italy. Cary Grant,

Adjø England

Bob Hope and Alistair Cooke are just three of the many Brits who quit the maternal shores and found fame in the USA.

An expat friend of ours puts it like this: "It's easy to say 'no' to new things, but far more interesting to find out what happens when you say 'yes'."

But let's be clear, there's nothing automatic about it. You don't instantly become a better, wiser, more spiritual – or richer – person simply by moving abroad. You don't inevitably change. But if you *want* to change you'll probably find it more possible in a new place. One thing in favour of going abroad is that it's very easy to become trapped by other people's expectations of you. If you try to change your life in Britain all the people you know start whispering things like 'mid-life crisis' or 'nervous breakdown'. Whereas, in a new place, nobody knows how you used to be. Maybe you want a less responsible job but can't face the idea of all your acquaintances saying that you've failed. Maybe you want to grow your hair and become an artist. Well, it worked for Gauguin.

Not everybody *can* make a new start in a different country. It just isn't in some people's psychological make-up, no matter how fed up they may get from time to time with their lives. How about you? Try this test. Tick the sentences that apply.

☐ You don't feel particularly British……

☐ You feel Britain has often been in the wrong…..

☐ Britain just doesn't offer the right kind of environment for a person like you…..

☐ Your standing in society is not important to you…..

Making a new start

☐ You believe people have to take responsibility for their own happiness…..

☐ You haven't yet discovered the real you…..

☐ You've discovered the real you but nobody else likes it…..

Score:
1-2 ticks: stay in Britain. 3-4 ticks: a new start might work. 5+ ticks: leave as soon as possible.

For every friend who has used moving abroad as some kind of life changing machine we have another stuck in exactly the same old rut but with a bit more sunshine.

One of our friends talks about his 'previous life' as if it was an earlier incarnation. He had been a draughtsman, spending his days drawing endless, tedious diagrams of tubes. Now he runs a guest house in the Pyrenees and works as a mountain guide. Another friend had his own factory employing 70 people. For 23 years he was a workaholic. Now he has a small riding school on the Costa Brava and lives very happily in a mobile home with his dogs, goats, chickens – and, of course, horses. These are people who have successfully made a fresh start and would never go back.

On the other hand, there's Tina from Birmingham who fell in love with a Catalan, moved to Spain to join him and is now exactly the same person doing exactly the same things as in Britain. And Jenny who was a solicitor in London and is now a *gestor* in Figueres (someone who sorts out other people's paperwork). That's not to say they haven't made fresh starts. They certainly have. But in their cases, the new life is much like the old one.

There are some things that a new start just can't change. If you have to pay money to your ex, you still have to even if you live in a new country. And don't go thinking that saying goodbye to Britain means saying goodbye to your outstanding tax bills. Tax is one thing you can never escape.

— Pros —

- Nobody need know anything about your past or the way you used to be.
- You can change things about yourself without anybody mumbling 'mid-life crisis'.
- Putting a bit of distance between yourself and a problem can throw it into perspective.
- If you haven't yet 'discovered yourself' exposure to new ideas and experiences may be just what you need.

— Cons —

- The pessimists say you can never run away from yourself.
- If you couldn't make a go of things in your own country it's going to be a whole lot harder in a new one.

— KEY QUESTIONS —

- Are you running away from something? If so, are you sure you're over it, or will you be bringing the baggage with you?
- Are you running towards something? If so, are you clear what it is? If not, are you sufficiently open to new ideas and influences to recognise the prize when you see it?
- Are you too set in your ways – too old, maybe – to change?

Finding new stimulation

— The Dream —

You're sitting in the famous Café des Phares on the Place de la Bastille, Paris, the very first of the *cafés philo*, founded in 1992. It's just after 11am on Sunday and the discussion is the future of capitalism. A few minutes earlier you were listening to that tragic Jacques Brel song *Ne Me Quitte Pas*. That tradition of *chanson* barely known in Britain. So unusual, with words that really mean something. So thought provoking. So, yes, stimulating. Through the smoke of a hundred Gauloises, Eric, a *soixante-huitard*, with the scar from a badly aimed cobblestone to prove his involvement in the student riots, announces the imminent fall of the capitalist system. Just as he did 35 years ago. Now the moderator is looking at you. This is the moment you've been waiting for. You take another swig of absinthe, the tipple of philosophers and artists, stand up and begin your polemic.

— The Reality —

If intellectual discussion is the kind of stimulation you're looking for then France is the country for you. Especially Paris. More than any other nation, the French make heroes out of philosophers. Bernard-Henri Lévy, for example, is a celebrity. Not only that, he's also rich with at least three homes, including an 18th century palace in Marrakech, once owned by John Paul Getty. So famous that you only have to say BHL to French intellectuals and they'll know who you mean.

At a party on one occasion we were approached by a French woman who, without any preliminaries about the weather, immediately demanded: 'Don't you think Cynicism is just like Buddhism?' We were completely floored. Philosophy is an obligatory subject in French schools, not an eccentricity, and there are now 160 *cafés philo* in France compared with only 70 in all the rest of the world put together. The British tradition of anti-intellectualism is very different.

But once again the problem of language rears up. It's hard enough grappling with philosophical concepts in your own language let alone a foreign one. Would you, for example, agree with existentialists who argue that phenomenology is also ontology? Now try it in French. Even people who would consider themselves fluent are left struggling. Where we live we have some French friends who are very definitely intellectuals – an arts correspondent for a major French newspaper, an artist, the owner of an art gallery, an anthropologist… and we just can't talk to them. At least, not on the level they enjoy amongst themselves. It just makes us feel so stupid. Far from feeling stimulated, we feel frustrated and inferior.

Finding new stimulation

For the same reason there's not much point in going to the theatre. Nor to the cinema, where the current vogue for mumbling lines may well be realistic but doesn't do anything for people who are wrestling with the language. Nor to any kinds of evening classes or courses if the subject is at all technical.

And this sense of being overawed doesn't just apply to intellectual life. All kinds of things you might have a go at in Britain just seem so overwhelming in a foreign country. Take something as simple as travelling by train. The need to specify the ticket in a foreign language, get it 'validated' in one of those funny machines and then find the right platform all turn something routine into a minor ordeal.

Or consider embarking on a new project. Having your own vineyard, for example. Well, Sting and Gerard Depardieu have done it, so why not you? You know the fantasy. You and your friends gathered in a happy, chattering group. The sun shining. The straw hats. Working your way along the rows, dropping the plump, purple bunches into wicker baskets. Pausing now and then for a mouthful of bread, a handful of olives and a swig of wine.

We'll say nothing of the fact that, in reality, it's incredibly hard, back breaking, wasp stung work. What we want to point out are the almost insurmountable obstacles to any project like this when you're in a strange country. You'd probably feel comfortable about buying a field in the UK. But will you be so confident in France or Spain or Italy? Will you need permission to clear the land for a vineyard? How do you register for any subventions going? What varieties do well? Can you join the local co-operative? Where can you buy bottles? And corks? What about the health regulations? Will you have to pay tax? And so on and so on. We're not saying you can't do it. Sure you can. It's just that, whatever the project, it's all so much more difficult than it would have been back in the UK.

Of course, you can argue that the difficulties are precisely what makes life abroad so stimulating. But, on the other hand, lots of expats are so overwhelmed they actually end up doing *less* than they did in the UK. We know quite a few who, far from being stimulated, simply don't know what to do with their lives. They develop a little routine in which they feel safe and stick to it. They don't throw themselves into any of the new things on offer. They go for pointless drives to pass the time. They shop in the same half dozen shops. They fill up their days with boozy lunches in the bars where the Brits gather and their nights with even boozier dinners. They form British societies. They speak to one another – in English. And that's about it.

Even those who master the language and the bureaucracy and are gracefully at ease in their new country can still fall into a kind of torpor. It's the Mediterranean climate, you see. The UK climate is conducive to rushing about doing things and being, well, stimulated. The Mediterranean climate, on the other hand, is so often conducive to doing absolutely nothing. Just sitting in the sun, watching the world go by and contemplating. Well, not even contemplation, actually, so much as reverie. Even vacancy.

Still, don't they say you first have to empty your mind before you can learn the secret of the universe?

Finding new stimulation

— Pros —

- ☼ Any change is bound to be stimulating.
- ☼ Certain cities of mainland Europe are renowned for their intellectual life — Paris, in particular.
- ☼ You'll experience all kinds of things you never would have done in the UK, from unusual wildlife (bearded vultures, beavers, ibex) to *Modernisme* architecture.

— Cons —

- ☂ A strange environment might make you more fearful of searching out the unfamiliar.
- ☂ Europe is all much of a muchness nowadays and far less stimulating than it used to be.
- ☂ Language problems are a hindrance to learning new things.
- ☂ You can find plenty of stimulation without leaving the UK.

— KEY QUESTIONS —

- Are you sure you have the energy to cope with all those new ideas and experiences?
- Are you the sort of person who will rise to the challenge and not be overwhelmed by it?
- Have you got the language skills to grapple with intellectual life in a foreign country?

An affordable dream home

— The Dream —

You've sold your house in London, paid off the mortgage and trousered a cool £350,000 in cash. Now you're off to find a new life abroad, unburdened by debt. You spend a glorious fortnight touring Portugal and, one day, you find exactly what you've been looking for. A development of modern houses on a golf course with the use of a shared swimming pool and health spa. What's more, it's so reasonable you can pay outright and still have cash left over. You sign up. The developer pays careful attention to your special requirements and three months later, right on schedule, you're moving into your dream home.

An affordable dream home

– The Reality –

So are house prices actually any cheaper in, say, France or Portugal or Greece than they are in the UK? Well how about this for example? A detached house right on the beach, with four bedrooms and its own boathouse for just £275,000? Now compare that with a three bedroom property and (instead of a boathouse) a one bedroom guesthouse on an estate of 15 at £3 million. There's no comparison, you say. Yes, well, the boathouse job is in the UK – more specifically Scotland. And the estate house is on Majorca.

The fact is that if you're selling a house in London or the south-east you'll be able to buy an equivalent property in the rural parts of France, Portugal, Spain, Italy or Greece for far less money. Or, equally, in the more remote parts of the UK, too. On the other hand, if you want to go where the millionaires sun themselves, the outer reaches of London might actually be cheaper. Yes, *cheaper*.

Let's take a look at what's been happening to house prices abroad:

- *France* is still a country of boom and bust – the peak of 1981/the bust of 1983, the peak of 1987/the bust of 1989, the peak of 1991/the bust of 1997. In 2003 prices were moving up an average of 15 percent. What everyone wants to know now is when the next bust is coming.

- *Italy* enjoyed a boom in the late 80s which was followed by the bust of 1993-96 when prices fell 15 percent in real terms. In 2003 prices went up an average of 10 percent while the areas most in demand, like Tuscany, reached 15 percent. But the growth rate has been slowing since.

Adiós Inglaterra

- *Spain* saw prices decline in real terms during most of the 90s, but economic growth, immigration and the purchase of second homes then started a boom which shows no sign of stopping yet. Prices have been moving up an average of 18 percent a year, with Madrid at the top of the league, the Costa del Sol and Costa Blanca on a more modest 5-10 percent and Majorca on zero.
- *Portugal* experienced an average 7 percent rise in house prices in 2003 while the Algarve and the Lisbon coastal area reached 10 percent. Price rises slowed markedly in 2004.
- *Greece* was slow to remove restrictions on foreign ownership and the pent-up demand fuelled annual price rises which have recently been as high as 30 percent in the most popular areas. An average of 6 percent growth is expected in each of the next few years.

Broadly, there are two ways of buying a dream home abroad.
- You can buy a house that already exists.
- You can buy a house that has yet to be built.

Of the two methods, the latter is the one that gives the most problems.

Selling property 'off the plan' (in other words, it hasn't been built yet) isn't a trick and isn't specifically designed to catch foreigners. Local people also buy this way and it can make a lot of sense. You sign a contract at a fixed price for a home you can't move into for, say, six months. So by the time it's ready it's worth (with luck) considerably more than you're paying.

Spanish friends of ours bought an apartment off the plan and moved in just recently. They're very happy, not least because they made a nice profit – on paper. But the process certainly wasn't with-

An affordable dream home

out its problems. The apartment was finished late (so they had to stay at a relative's in the meantime). And many of their stipulations regarding options and extras were either ignored or misinterpreted. Every week during the building there was a battle over something. And, don't forget, this was a Spanish couple. Buying off the plan and making the occasional trip from England to check progress you're almost *bound* to have problems.

Nor is the potential for disputes any less in the more exclusive developments where buyers are often tied up in all kinds of restrictive clauses. For example, any improvements you want subsequently may have to be carried out by the developers rather than a contractor of your own choosing. So whose dream house is it, anyway? Our advice is: *don't sign.*

In fact, according to one survey[4], nearly 60 percent of British people buying property in Spain believe they have been misled at some point. The same percentage feel that estate agents understated the full cost of buying and owning property in Spain. And nearly three quarters bemoaned the impossibility of getting independent advice. However, the good news is that only 3 percent were unhappy to have bought in Spain.

Part of the problem is that in countries like Spain, Italy and France, property transactions are handled by a notary, a public servant whose principal function is to collect tax for the government. So you won't find the notary much help on things like rights of way across the property, or the connection of drains, or other developments that might block the view.

---

[4] Inmueble and Spanish Property Insight (www.spanish-property-insight.com).

On the other hand you can consult any notary for advice on property matters (not necessarily the one acting in the sale) and if you have any problems you should obviously do this well in advance of signing.

Everyone advises you to get your own lawyer. Well, that's the case in some countries but not in all. On one occasion, following the advice, we went to an *abogado*, a Spanish lawyer. He looked at us in astonishment. "But what do you want me to *do*?" he asked, spreading his hands in bewilderment. "Well," we said, "we don't know. We thought you did." It turned out that never in his life before had he been asked to get involved in a property transaction. The fact is that land and house purchases aren't treated with the same awe as in Britain. You don't have all that rigmarole for a car so why for a house?

Find out what the locals do and copy them. Even if you have a lawyer we'd still suggest you do your best to check everything for yourself with the help of a local friend or an expat who speaks the language and has already been through the process. We'd also advise:

- Never go on a trip organised by a developer.
- Never accept hospitality from a developer.
- Never sign up to any clauses that restrict your rights as a freeholder.
- Never do anything that would be crazy in Britain – like buy a timeshare from someone who approaches you in the street.

When it comes to an existing property you may have to tangle with the thorny old question of 'black'. That is, in order to reduce tax liabilities, a vendor may want to declare a sale price well below the

An affordable dream home

actual price so that you pay the rest under the table. The standard advice is not to do it. Very sensible. The only problem is that, very often, you simply won't be able to buy your dream home otherwise. It's as simple as that.

Most people who have bought property in the Mediterranean can tell you funny stories about this. The way the notary suddenly has to dash out of the office for five minutes – which gives you the time to hand over the brown envelope. It's a way of life.

The declared price also has a bearing on costs. In Italy, for example, the registration fees for a house are 11 percent of the *declared* sales price. In other words, declare 300,000 euros and you'll pay 33,000 euros. Declare 200,000 euros and you'll pay 22,000 euros. In Greece purchase costs can be as high as 18 percent.

So how *do* you go about it all? The most important thing is *don't rush*. Maybe you risk losing a property but there will always be plenty of others. Don't talk to just one agent, talk to lots of agents. If you're interested in a new unit in a particular development speak to people who already live there. Ask them if their unit was completed on time, at the agreed price and to the agreed specification. And, of course, talk to the town hall about developments in the area. A lot of places are changing very fast. What you see today is not what you'll be seeing out of your windows next year. Don't just see the area on a sunny spring day. Make sure you understand what it's like in the heat of the summer and the cold of winter and during a storm. It's not just money we're talking about. It's your dream. So work on it.

Personally, we would never buy 'off the plan' or buy from a developer. But that's us. We like to be able to see what we're getting before

Adiós Inglaterra

we part with any money. And if we wanted a brand new home we'd buy the land and get it built ourselves. There are always hard luck stories. But the reality is that most people buy with no more problems than they would have in England – and are generally far happier.

– Pros –

- Property prices in Mediterranean countries tend to be cheaper than in the UK.
- Property values in some areas abroad (especially parts of Greece and Spain) could grow faster than in the UK.
- Some of the new building systems are superior to those used in the UK.
- If you contract for a property not yet built the price should be fixed (make sure it is) and you stand to make an immediate profit the day you take possession.

– Cons –

- To benefit from low prices you have to 'discover' new areas – away from towns, beaches, ski resorts and tourist attractions. This may suit you, but it may not. If you dream of the same kind of house as most people – by the sea or in a ski resort – it probably won't be any cheaper than in the UK.
- Property abroad may go up in value more slowly than in the UK, making it difficult to move back later.
- The euro/sterling exchange rate may change unfavourably for your circumstances.
- Negotiations may have to be conducted in a foreign language.

An affordable dream home

– KEY QUESTIONS –

- Are you willing to take the risk of buying 'off the plan'? Do you have the time and money to make frequent trips to check progress? Do you have the money available to put down on a property not yet built? If not, consider buying a property already completed.
- Does it have to be a brand new house or apartment, anyway? Will a slightly used one be acceptable? In some cases, second hand homes (like second hand cars) are cheaper than new ones.
- Do you know what other developments might be taking place around you in the future?
- Have you checked to see what liability you might have for the cost of things like the development of roads and street lighting?
- Are you fully aware of the total purchase costs? They can be as high as 18 percent in Greece, for example.

12

Being near sunny beaches

— The Dream —

You've finished work for the day but it's still hot. What you need is to head for the beach to cool off. When you arrive at your secret cove the few tourists who know about it are already packing up. Good! This is the time of day for the locals. Only 15 minutes after leaving work you're already streaking down the beach and plunging into the warm, limpid water. It feels so good. You swim 100 metres flat out to the floating platform, haul yourself aboard and lie sunbathing. Back home you and your partner have dinner on the terrace. The sun has dropped well below the horizon, the stars are out and the moon will soon be rising. "Fancy some skinny dipping?" you suggest.

Being near sunny beaches

— The Reality —

In summer there are no deserted beaches left anywhere in Europe. If you're the kind of person who likes a crowded beach – and plenty of people do – then you're in luck. But if you're the sort of person who dreams of empty, unspoiled expanses of white sand you're going to have to look further afield.

Beach resorts are places of enormous contrasts. In winter they can be so dead that the few year round residents start contemplating suicide. Most of the shops are closed, the supermarket is boarded up, the apartments all have their shutters down and locked, the beach is covered in debris and the palm trees are shrouded in plastic against the winter storms. Then in summer they're so crowded that, yes, you contemplate suicide all over again. The prices in the shops have doubled. You can't get a table at your favourite restaurant (and even if you could the food and service would be awful). The roads are jammed with cars and the cars are stuffed with irritable people and their half-inflated beach toys.

Houses near the sea take a tremendous battering. The salt air corrodes metalwork while salt crystals tend to jam up mechanical things like roller blinds. The salt laden wind plays havoc with the paintwork which has to be redone every year. Inside, furnishings are constantly damp in winter and there's mould on the walls. Outside, gardening is an unending struggle against the elements.

With all these disadvantages you'd think property would be cheap near a beach. Not a bit of it. A sea view will cost you at least double the price of an equivalent property inland. And if you want the first rank – actually on the beach – you could pay three or four times more for the privilege of having your home battered by winter storms.

Let's face it, even in southern Europe the beach season isn't that long. The water is pretty cold until June and the sun is pretty weak after the middle of September. For year round beaches you need the Canary Islands or, better still, the Caribbean.

People who live from tourists have to make their money during this short season, which means that for a few weeks a year prices are astronomical. Once the season is underway you suddenly realise your shopping bill is 50 percent higher than normal. So you can't use the local shops any more but have to drive to the supermarket in the nearest inland town.

There's also a more serious side to seasonal overcrowding. Sewage plants are often so overwhelmed that raw sewage ends up being pumped into that idyllic little bay in front of your windows. And medical facilities are so packed with tourists being treated for sunburn and jellyfish stings that you can't get your own problems attended to.

Work can be a lottery. Because of the cyclical nature of a beach resort there's too much in summer and not enough in winter. If your work is connected with tourism you'll find yourself too exhausted in summer to enjoy the beach or even go there. Come the winter you'll have plenty of time (you may even be out of work till next season). But by then the beach has lost its attraction.

Social life can be a trial. You'll probably know plenty of people who only stay for a few weeks a year. As soon as they arrive they want to 'play'. They're on holiday but you're not. You pass a hectic time with

Being near sunny beaches

far more late nights than you can manage and too much alcohol. When they leave you sigh with relief – but the next group is coming tomorrow. The same applies to relatives and friends who want to come and stay with you. Normal routine goes to pot. On the other hand, come winter, the place is deserted and you have no social life at all.

– Pros –

- A sea view is romantic and inspiring. Even winter storms can be enjoyable.
- Summer temperatures are that little bit lower on the coast and there's always at least a touch of a breeze – an important consideration in the Mediterranean region.
- A beach close by is wonderful for kids. They never have to ask: "What can we do now?"
- Winter temperatures will be just that little bit milder than inland – an important consideration for the garden.

– Cons –

- Property prices are much higher on the coast than inland, especially when there's a sea view and even more so if the property is actually on the beach.
- Sea air and winter storms involve constant and expensive maintenance.
- Although winters may be milder than inland the high humidity by the sea can make temperatures *seem* lower and be detrimental for rheumatism and some other conditions.
- The beach life means an increased risk of skin cancer.

Adjö England

- Beach resorts tend to be dead in winter, overcrowded in summer and just right only briefly.
- The coast road is one long traffic jam in summer.
- A beach can be a constant source of worry when you have children.

– KEY QUESTIONS –

- Can you afford the cost of property near the beach? Would you prefer a larger property inland for the same money?
- Are you prepared for the extra maintenance involved in a seaside house?
- Will you really go to the beach very often? Maybe a pool would be a better bet.
- Does the 'boom-bust' annual cycle of a beach resort bother you – deserted in winter, overcrowded in summer? Would you prefer a town or village inland where there's a year round sense of community?
- Do you have any medical conditions that might be exacerbated by the damp in winter?

Personal growth

— The Dream —

Everybody would like to be a better person tomorrow than they are today. And you're no different. Yet it's so difficult living in the UK, commuting to work and just being another rat in the rat race. There simply isn't the time to do much more than survive. At one time you thought money was everything. Now you know better. The life you dream about would be so different. There'd be the time to learn flamenco guitar and an old gypsy to learn it from. The time to study philosophy. The time for Tao, Tai Chi and Shiatsu. The time for contemplation and meditation. The time for discovering your own inner voice. But it's not just a question of time. Moving abroad would mean opening your mind to new ideas and a different way of looking at things. Above all it would also be a challenge and it's only through facing up to challenges that you can ever really grow.

Allahaismarladik İngiltere

— The Reality —

As Zorba the Greek put it in that thought provoking book by Kazantzakis, you need a little madness otherwise you never dare cut the cord and be free. Leaving your parents is an important step on the road to personal growth. Leaving your country is an even bigger one.

And yet. And yet. Thanks to the EU you can now live in many other European countries without altogether cutting ties with the UK. It's a bit like being at university and taking your washing home at weekends. You set up house in Greece or Italy or Portugal or wherever but when you hit a real problem it's to Britain and British people that you turn. Involved in a dispute over a property purchase? Get a British lawyer. Suffering from a tricky health problem? Nip back to the old country for the NHS to sort it out.

And as we've been arguing all through the book, moving to another EU country isn't really *that* different from living in the UK. It's a challenge but nowhere near as big a challenge as it used to be. Nor can you point to anything about another EU country that's more conducive to personal growth than remaining in the UK. Granted, new experiences must result in a degree of personal development. But it would be pretty difficult to exhaust the possibilities that already exist. What could be more challenging than, say, working with teenage offenders in a British inner city? Or helping AIDS victims? Especially if you're moving – which is normally the plan – to a place in Europe where life is more agreeable. After all, if you're a middle class, liberal minded person now you'll probably mix with middle class, liberal minded people abroad. You'll get a more dramatically different angle by mixing with, say, British aristocrats or

Personal growth

miners. Why should personal growth be the result of living in a nice house with a swimming pool, joining friends for al fresco meals at the beach and going skiing at weekends?

How do you define or measure personal growth anyway? For some it all seems to be inexorably involved with Oriental philosophies and ideas. In which case it might be more logical to move to India or China. Failing that it could be better to remain somewhere like Finchley where all those self improvement courses are so popular – shamanism, Chi-Nei-Tsang, Feng Shui, Tao, Tantra, holo this and holo that, shiatsu, kiatsu and all the rest of it. At least you'll be receiving instruction in English. How are you going to achieve enlightenment if you can only understand one word in three?

If you take the view that personal growth comes less from instruction and more from periods of isolation and self-examination then, yes, mainland Europe certainly does have a lot of possibilities, given the belief that spiritual growth increases with altitude. Think of Montserrat in Spain, Mount Athos in Greece, and La Verna in Tuscany where St Francis of Assisi (another hilltop village) founded the Convento della Verna and later received the Stigmata there. If you want to sit up a mountain there's no argument that the Continent has more possibilities – around the Mediterranean you can actually *live* a thousand metres higher than Britain's highest peak. And in the same way that a retreat gets you away from other, possibly negative, influences, so moving abroad takes you away from the environment that moulded you in a way that, perhaps, you don't care for. But on the other hand, you can't get much further away from things than an uninhabited island in the Outer Hebrides.

Speaking for ourselves, the activity that has caused the most personal growth since leaving the UK has been training horses. Which we learned in France and Spain. It may sound a bit crazy if you've had nothing to do with such beasts and never wanted to. But a horse holds up a mirror to you. In other words, if you want your horse to be kind, composed and calm you first have to learn how to be those things yourself. It's Oriental philosophy in practice. Of course, you can train horses in the UK. But we never did. It was the weather and the mountains that got us on horseback. In the UK we probably wouldn't ride. But many others do.

So what are we left with in favour of mainland Europe? Not a lot. But as with Ithaka, it's not so much the arriving as the journey itself. You'll be moving from a place you know and consider you belong, to a place you don't know where others may say you don't belong. A sort of rebirthing, if you like. And maybe that is the very essence of personal growth – learning to see conflicts from someone else's side.

You'll certainly get a different view of Britain when abroad because you'll hear it from everybody around you. Quite frankly, Britain isn't too popular on the mainland of Europe right now. It's, to say the least, out of step with popular opinion, certainly in the rest of Western Europe.

Generally speaking, criticisms of Britain, valid or not, won't necessarily be held against you personally (especially not if you happen to agree with them). But you'll no longer be living in a society in which British people (i.e. you) are always right. In which British people (i.e. you) are considered to be more important than anybody else. Instead you'll be hearing – possibly on the local TV news – that the British (i.e. you) are the bad guys. That's already quite interesting for personal growth.

Personal growth

It's pretty sobering to realise that at one time or another Britain has been involved in hostilities with just about every country in Europe (not to say the world) – and some people still haven't forgotten. France, Spain, Italy, Austria, Bulgaria, Germany, Hungary, Romania, Slovakia, Turkey… the list goes on and on. And on. Don't forget that, one way or another, the British Empire once engulfed a quarter of the globe. And a quarter of its population. And there are plenty of people who don't look back very fondly on it. Foreigners, basically.

Can it really be that the French have changed so much we no longer have to fight them? And the Spanish? And the Italians? And the Austrians? And the Germans? And all the rest. It must all mean something. But what? More to ponder as you reach for personal growth.

– Pros –

- Moving abroad can give you a whole new perspective on your life – and your country of birth.
- Exposure to new places, people and ideas must inevitably expand horizons.
- A new place tends to create an atmosphere of change in your personal life as well.
- Putting some distance between yourself and 'negative' influences can give you the space to break out of prejudices.

Allahaismarladik İngiltere

— Cons —

- ☂ Europe doesn't provide the kind of challenge it did when the Wife of Bath set out for Santiago de Compostela.
- ☂ It could be more of a challenge to remain in Britain with its awful weather and, according to some, its equally awful political and economic situation.
- ☂ There are just as many opportunities for personal growth in Britain as elsewhere, and probably far more in a big city like London than in a small village or resort in mainland Europe.

— KEY QUESTIONS —

- What do you actually mean by personal growth? Has it got to do with developing characteristics like kindness and wisdom or with lots of new accomplishments (playing the bouzouki, learning shiatsu, grappling with Existentialism?). Either way, won't learning and comprehension come more easily in the UK where you can understand the language?
- Will your new circumstances abroad (settling in, grappling with the regulations, earning a living) really leave you more time for personal growth than you had in the UK?
- Are you really the sort of person willing to look at things from someone else's perspective? If not, conflicts are more likely to reinforce your prejudices than remove them – you'll end up more British abroad than you were at home.

14

Restoring an old ruin

— The Dream —

An avenue of trees leads up to it. As the building comes into view you see a broad expanse of gravel, wide steps leading to the front door, turrets, rows of windows with shutters, even a stable block that could become your studio. It's a chateau. And it could all be yours. Yours for the price of a semi in Neasden. Of course, it needs a little bit of work. You'd have to expect that for the price. The roof has a problem. Most of it is missing. But if it wasn't you could hardly afford it, could you? When all the work is finished in a few months (you didn't get where you are by wasting time) you'll have a property that any aristocrat who survived the Revolution would be proud of. And it'll be worth a pile, too.

Αντίο Αγγλία

— The Reality —

You've already missed the boat in all the popular parts of Spain, France and Italy. Ten years ago you could have bought a ruined farmhouse in Spain for, maybe, £5,000. Even five years ago the price might have been £25,000. But now you'll be lucky to find anything under £60,000. And we are talking ruins here, not just dilapidated. A few years back all the country folk were heading for the towns. They wanted jobs where you didn't have to get up at 5am, as well as houses with central heating and inside toilets. Nobody wanted the countryside. Now everything has changed. Town bred foreigners from northern Europe have decided that squalor is picturesque and are fighting over everything the 'peasants' have abandoned.

Even so, prices are still lower than in the UK, basically because the population density in France is less than half that of the UK, while Spain (and Greece) are only one third. And there's more good news. When you're buying a ruin the price is almost irrelevant. You want to know why? Because it will be utterly dwarfed by the cost of renovation.

The snag, you see, is that buying a ruin is only the first of many payments before your dream becomes reality. You need materials to put your ruin in order. You need bricks, stones, tiles, window frames, doors, plaster, electric cable… the list goes on and on…and on. And in most of Europe these things tend to cost about the same as in Britain.

Then you need labour. In France that costs about the same as in Britain; in Spain, Portugal and Greece a bit less. But not that much. And if there are specialist skills involved (like building in stone) that may cost extra.

Restoring an old ruin

But surely, you say to yourself as you stroll around an ancient stone built *mas*, I could just pile the rocks back into place myself? And they won't cost a thing, because they're just lying around in the fields. Well, believe us, the cheapest way of completing those tumble down walls is in brick. Yes, brick. It's a crime, but people do it. Then hide the scene of the crime under a layer of render. The cheapest – and most sensible option of all – is to knock everything down and start again with modern materials.

But, then, you're not buying a ruin because you're sensible. You're doing it because you're mad. (Well, it certainly helps.) This will give you an idea. We bought a stone water mill dating from the 16th century for the equivalent of £25,000, together with five acres of land. It was only a small mill as these things go – about 100 square metres on the ground floor. At the end of two years, using local builders and tradesmen (we're not very handy) we'd run through about £250,000. We have a beautiful home vastly superior to anything we could have afforded in the south-east of England. But, it's *not* vastly superior to houses we could have afforded in, say, Yorkshire or Scotland.

There are three basic ways of getting your dream home done up:
- Employ a large building firm on an impressive looking, fixed price contract.
- Employ the small, village builder.
- Do it yourself (assuming you have the skills, and the regulations allow).

It's very hard to meet any couple who are happy with their builder. This has something to do with builders but far more, actually, to do with clients. Clients (you) have quite unrealistic expectations. And quite unrealistic fears.

Αντίο Αγγλία

It works like this. You ask the builder for a fixed price. After all, it sounds sensible. But how can he possibly know how many beams are rotten, how much mortar has been washed out of the middle of the wall over the years or how much rock there is where the septic tank will go before he actually starts work? It just isn't possible. So he has two choices. To quote a large sum which will cover all eventualities, but lose him the job. Or to quote the smaller sum he knows you'll accept and hope you can come up with more money if necessary. When he opens up a section of stone wall and discovers – *Hostia!* – it's all crumbling to dust, what can he do? He has to ask you for more money. And what do you do? You can try insisting he stick to the price. But this is not a big enterprise. This is one man, his son and his cousin. If you don't pay them they'll starve. You *have* to pay them. So what was the point of the fixed price in the first place?

Our recipe is this. Ask for recommendations. Favour the local builder. The sort of small enterprise that was started by granddad, where dad is now the boss and the two sons do all the heavy work. Their livelihood depends on them guarding their local reputation.

When you find a builder you like, ask him to charge you by the hour. But, you gasp, how can I trust him to tell me the number of hours? OK. If you can't trust him to do that, *don't employ him*. You have to find someone you believe you can trust, and then trust him.

How do you find out if you can trust someone? By starting off with a small job. Every big project can be broken down into a series of steps. So start with the first. If that goes well, continue to the next job. And so on.

If you can't be present yourself throughout the work you're asking for trouble. The fact is that it's in the nature of renovating old build-

Restoring an old ruin

ings that something unforeseen will come up every day. Also, it's all very well looking at a plan, or even artists' impressions, but most people are not very good at envisaging how something will actually be. Almost certainly, as work proceeds and you see things taking shape, you'll get new ideas.

Do you want this door opening to the left or to the right? Do you want the stone jointed in concrete (very strong) or would you prefer the colour of the more traditional lime? Wouldn't it be better to put a shower here instead of a bath, otherwise there's barely room for the toilet? If you're not around to say what you want, the builder will be obliged to make a decision. If he's a good guy he will do his best. But it may not be what you want.

You have to allow, you see, for cultural differences. In our mill we had a terrible job getting the builder to construct the bathroom to the dimensions we wanted. To him, it was a waste of space. That was his heartfelt advice. We could gain, he pointed out, another bedroom which would make the house more valuable. (Yes, but an *empty* bedroom because we didn't need it.) He just didn't understand that we would want to lounge around in the bath listening to music.

Do you need an architect? The local planning authority may not give you the choice. But – unless you like having everything taken out of your hands – we suggest you keep his role to the minimum. Our builder, Liberto was his name, knew far more than the architect. Which made the architect a waste of money. Moreover, the architect wanted to do things *his* way, completely overlooking the fact that it was *our* house.

The architect didn't like slate around the shower. He felt sure we

Αντίο Αγγλία

meant marble. Slate would be too difficult to clean. Nor did he like this. Nor that. In the end we got our way on most things but it was hard work. Which just about sums up every aspect of the whole process.

But, one day, as you lie in your circular bath listening to your favourite CD, a glass of wine in your hand, the light from the wood burning stove making patterns on the ceiling, you'll reflect that, yes, maybe you were mad. But not to have done it would have been a whole lot madder.

— Pros —

- If you've done everything right, and you can afford what's necessary, you'll end up with an enviable and unique home.
- There's immense satisfaction in putting your personal stamp on a building, having the space laid out to your particular needs, in seeing it brought back to life and — if this is your thing — knowing you're living in a house that has history.
- You'll acquire an intimate knowledge of house building, local people and unusual phrases, such as: *Anda ya!* (In your dreams!)

— Cons —

- The renovation is going to cost half as much again as you calculated.
- And take twice as long as you thought.
- At the end of it all, the property might be worth *less* than you've spent.
- You can't be sure what you're going to end up with, especially if the project is entirely in the hands of an architect and builders.
- If you're doing the work yourself you're going to be losing a lot of income and/or leisure time.

Restoring an old ruin

- Maybe, until the project is finished (one year, two, five?) you'll have to forego the very attractions that you actually came for (the beach, skiing, riding etc.).

> ### — KEY QUESTIONS —
>
> - What is it about the idea of renovating an old property that appeals to you? Might you be better with a property that's already been renovated? Or even a modern property?
> - Who is going to do the work? If it's you, do you have the skills? Or will it look like a bodge up and actually *reduce* the value of the property? Can you afford the time? Would it be better to keep the day job and let others do the work? If you have to rely on builders and other tradesmen, are they available? Will you be able to instruct them clearly in their own language?
> - Do you have enough money to buy the ruin and renovate it? So many people hopelessly underestimate.
> - Can you afford to have the entire renovation project completed at one go? If not, can you cope with living in a house which is constantly undergoing renovation? Or will you be living somewhere else? Where?
> - Have you really made a realistic appraisal of costs? Are you sure you're not just deluding yourself because you so much want to do this? Do you have a contingency fund? You're going to need it.

15

Becoming fluent in another language

— The Dream —

Some friends have come out from the UK to visit. As they sit, somewhat bewildered, at the restaurant table with you, you peruse the menu. What would they like? Perhaps prosciutto to start. They can probably work out what that is for themselves. But will they know gamberetti are shrimps? And what will they make of una braciola di maiale? You try not to smirk as you glance across at them. "Need any help with the menu?" Just then, somebody you know wanders past. "Buona sera," you say. "Come sta?" Then launch into conversation about the latest scandal in the village. Your friends' mouths hang open.

Becoming fluent in another language

— The Reality —

There's nothing automatic about becoming fluent just because you live in another country. Believe us. We lived in France for 10 years and we've been in Spain for five. We're far from fluent in either language. On the other hand, we have a friend called Kevin who speaks French like a native. And another friend called Emma who speaks Spanish (Castilian) better than the majority of people in Catalonia where she now lives (apart from an incorrigible Scottish burr). The difference between them and us is that Kevin lives with a French woman and Emma lives with a Spanish man. That's the real way to learn.

But two British people living together, tuning in to the BBC and socialising with other Brits or, at least, other English speakers, isn't a recipe for success.

The fact is that anywhere in the world you can *get by* with a smattering of the language. And lots of people do. Take shopping, for example. Years ago you had to ask for things. Now you can go to the supermarket and just help yourself. At a restaurant there's a good chance the menu will be translated into English (or have pictures). And when you're really stuck there's usually someone around who speaks English.

In any event, experts say 85 percent of human communication is non-verbal. Things like *I don't agree* or *I'm angry* or *I'll take one of those* are all pretty clear without words.

Of course, there are times a smattering just isn't enough, but there's always a way round problems of that sort. When you need to write a letter or attend a meeting you can always get a friend to translate for you. As for social life, there are Brits living almost everywhere in Europe and, even if there aren't any near you, you can always at least find someone Dutch who speaks English as well as you do.

So is it really worth going to all that trouble for a mere 15 percent of communication which *is* verbal? Especially when most of the 15 percent concerns the more intimate things largely reserved for your partner, anyway.

Well, of course, intimacy is exactly the point. If you want to progress beyond the 'me no like' level of conversation with local people and really develop meaningful relationships with them, you need to speak the language properly. And that may also mean learning the local dialect. You'll always be an outsider, anyway, but if you don't speak like the locals you'll be so far out you'll be in space, with no real local friends.

Up till now we've been talking about just *living* abroad. If you're actually going to *work* in the country then fluency is essential. But, in that case, you can't really afford to wait till you get there.

For those who can wait, the key to success is to immerse yourself as totally as possible. If you're a couple, make it a rule that you'll speak to one another in the local language for an hour every evening. Watch local TV, not British TV. Even having local television or radio on in the background will help. You may not actually learn much but at least you'll get a feel for the sound of the language.

You'll probably find you'll reach a stage where you can understand quite a lot but not actually say anything. Men seem to get stuck at this stage more than women, probably because communication is generally more important to the female sex.

Becoming fluent in another language

Quite often, following a conversation with somebody in the village, we'll come away both having the same impression of what the conversation was about but with exactly opposite views about what the person actually meant. At the end of the day, it can all come down to one tiny, momentary sound that makes all the difference. For example, one of us will think the speaker said we could have planning permission and the other that the speaker said we couldn't. One of us will think the mayor said he did like the porch we'd built and the other that he didn't. It can be very frustrating. The right way, of course, is to say when you don't understand – tedious but essential.

Obviously it's a good idea to take lessons. But don't imagine that, say, two one hour lessons per week *on their own* are going to take care of the problem. Rather, use them to understand grammar and deal with specific problems. Most of the learning still needs to be done by you.

Sometimes we tape record important telephone conversations. They're the hardest of all. Then we can listen to them again to make sure we understood.

One of the greatest inventions for learning language has got to be the DVD. Any film that was originally in English is always sold abroad with English as one of the available languages. If you live in Spain, for example, you'll be able to watch in English first, then Spanish (and you can also choose Spanish or English subtitles). It works best when you watch a sequence of just ten minutes over and over again, rather than the whole movie. Unfortunately, the Spanish version won't be a direct translation of the English and we find the subtitles bear only a vague resemblance to the actual dialogue. But it's an enormous help.

Another really terrific aid is the language course on CD-ROM. Not only do you hear the correct pronunciation but you can also record your own answers and compare them.

Here are some more ideas:
- Listen to local TV and radio as much as possible. Advertisments are great as they're so repetitive.
- Read a local newspaper.
- Read comics.
- Read children's books.
- Repeat phrases to yourself while you're doing the housework or cutting the grass.
- Write down the words and phrases you learn to help fix them in your brain. Just hearing them isn't enough.
- Buy a dictionary or phrasebook of slang – that's what most people will be speaking.

Of course, there's a huge difference between children and adults. Experts say the cut-off is around 10 years of age. Before that children can easily absorb the language just by hearing it. Older children and adults, alas, have to learn in a more structured (and tedious) sort of way. We have more to say about this in the chapter *A Better Place To Bring Up Children*. Basically, young children are no problem provided they're totally immersed in the foreign language. Some friends of ours who have been living in Spain for just over two years use their children to translate for them.

In our questionnaire we asked people: "What would you do differently another time?" Quite a few answered they wished they'd made more effort to learn the language before leaving Britain. It's all very well to assume you'll pick it up when you get there, but what are you

Becoming fluent in another language

going to do in the meantime? You may spend several miserable months.

Above all, don't give up. It's widely agreed that British people just can't learn foreign languages but that's just a cop out. Richard Burton (the explorer, not the actor) was fluent in at least 25 languages and could learn a new one in about two months. So there.

— Pros —

- There's no better way to learn a language than total immersion in the country where it's spoken.

— Cons —

- Living abroad is no guarantee of learning a language – it's too easy to get by without speaking it.
- You'll probably still have to pay for lessons if you want to make real progress.
- Nowadays, there are plenty of other ways of learning, including CD-ROM language courses and foreign language DVDs.

— KEY QUESTIONS —

- Is learning naturally in the country really just code for 'can't be bothered to make an effort'? If so, you still won't make much progress.
- Do you need to hit the ground running – for work, for example? If so, you can't really afford to defer learning until you get there.

Being near ski slopes

— The Dream —

1pm. The sky is blue. Snow is dripping rhythmically from the roof. You've completed a good morning's work. You deserve a break. You could take the Saint Martin 1 and 2 chairlifts to Tougnete, ski down to Meribel, buy a basket of chips for lunch, take the Tougnete gondola, ski back down to Saint Martin and still be at your desks by 3pm. Why not? Half an hour later the two of you are standing at nearly 2,500 metres, the Belleville valley laid out to the west and with Meribel a long, fast descent through pine trees below you. The pistes are quiet because most skiers are at lunch. But you haven't been practising all winter just to stay on the piste. With a whoop you pick up speed, carve a series of turns to get in rhythm, then swoop over the lip and into the deep snow between the trees, throwing up a white spray as you go.

— The Reality —

We lived an entire winter in *Les 3 Vallées*, which bills itself as the largest ski domain in the world, and another winter in Gavarnie, a ski resort in the Central Pyrenees. It was *great* both times. But we had the huge advantage of freelance contracts to write about what we were doing. Having the luxury of four months in the mountains we never skied when it was snowing, or windy, or cloudy. We literally could decide to slip out skiing for a few hours whenever we liked. That's not the situation for people with more regular jobs. More usually you have to work when the lifts are running and only get time off when the station is closed.

In *Les 3 Vallées* we lived in a little agricultural village just above the resort of Saint Martin de Belleville. It was the at end of the road with the smell of cowsheds in the air. Each morning we went to the farm for a jug of fresh milk to make the coffee to wash down the dark local bread thickly spread with the local honey. To us it was the best of both worlds. We lived in tranquillity with the world's most extensive network of lifts and runs at our feet.

In Gavarnie it was the same story. The ski station was separate from the village, which meant we weren't much bothered by tourists but could still get into the lift system pretty quickly when we wanted.

But we didn't live in either of these villages year round. And that's a big difference. Because ski resorts out of season can be pretty horrible. By April the snow is no longer white but a dirty grey and as the mantle recedes so it reveals last autumn's rubbish, the piles of building rubble and the heaps of manure. The grass is flat and yellow and won't take on that succulent green for several weeks. The ground is boggy with meltwater. And as the temperature rises so the moisture evaporates and huge clouds engulf everything, blotting out the sun for days on end. And once the snow has all gone the lifts look simply hideous and the runs appear as ugly scars on the mountainside.

It's no use living in a ski resort if skiing is the only mountain activity you like. Because for most of the year you can't ski. A low altitude resort may only provide reasonable snow three months of the year, and even a high altitude resort will only give you five months (unless there's a glacier for summer skiing). If you also like climbing, canyoning, mountain biking, hiking and horse riding then great. If not, you could be pretty bored.

Unless you've been clever enough to find yourself a secluded little backwater the constant stream of tourists could start to become annoying. The roads are going to be crowded (especially on changeover day). Prices in the local shops, bars and restaurants are going to be far higher than normal. You can manage during a holiday but you'll be bankrupted if you shop locally every week of the year.

Fairly obviously, life up a mountain can be *cold*. Your heating bills will be enormous. At night and early in the morning it might be, say, minus 10. It has to be said that because the air is dry you don't notice it the way you would in Britain. But even so, you need to be well equipped. An old banger of a car is going to be a liability. What's more, when people down at the coast are enjoying the spring you'll still be in the middle of winter. They'll be admiring the colours of the flowers and you'll still be looking out on a desert of white. The winter starts earlier, too, up

Being near ski slopes

the mountain. In other words, the summer is short and the winter long.

In the morning you have to spend 15 minutes clearing your windscreen (unless, of course, you have a garage). And several times a year you'll have to dig your car out of the snow. You'll be well advised to get a 4WD and at the very least snow tyres. If you don't have 4WD you'll be obliged to put chains on for the snow (then take them off when you go down to the valley, then put them on again when you come up – tedious and very cold).

Generally speaking, flat building land is scarce in the mountains and building materials are at a premium because of the delivery costs. The result is that houses and apartments tend to be small and expensive. If you've ever rented a holiday flat in one of the newer French blocks you'll know what we mean. More than once we've taken a holiday apartment described as suitable for 'up to six people' which was barely civilised for two – a bedroom so small there was almost no room to stand beside the bed. You can put up with it for a week but not for life.

If it's what you love, a ski resort can be the greatest place in the world. But it certainly isn't for everybody. If we were going back to the mountains now – and we're talking about it – we'd try to find somewhere hidden away but not more than 30 minutes from a resort. But that's just us.

— Pros —

- You can ski all season.
- A season's lift pass doesn't cost much more than a two week pass.
- You'll be living in or near a tourist destination with all the extra facilities such as swimming pool, outdoor jacuzzi, nightlife and restaurants.
- The climate at altitude is pretty much ideal as far as many people are concerned. You always feel vigorous. Winters are cold but normally sunny because you're higher than the clouds. And in summer you escape the debilitating heat of the coast.

— Cons —

- All that snow, which looks so good on a postcard, can get tedious when you have to live with it several months a year.
- Living costs are far higher than down on the plain.
- The majority of the year there is no skiing. When there is skiing the resort and the pistes are horribly crowded.
- In small resorts with no suitable schools children have to be bussed down to the valley every day – or maybe board.
- At altitude the summer is short.
- Work in a ski resort tends to be seasonal.
- Life can be hard above the snowline. You need to be fit, self-reliant and well equipped.

– KEY QUESTIONS –

- Do you know what your chosen resort is like out of season? In the autumn? In the late spring? In the summer?
- Is skiing the only mountain activity you enjoy? If so, what will you do the rest of the year?
- Can you find suitable work in a ski resort?
- Can you afford the premium that in ski resorts goes on everything from the price of a chalet to the cost of milk?
- Are you prepared for the time it takes to get down the mountain before you can start to go anywhere?
- Are you the kind of person who can dig a car out of the snow, fix snow chains in a blizzard and split logs?
- Do you want to live where there is normally permanent snow in winter (romantic but hard work) or would you be better off a little lower where you can get to the snow when you want but life is easier?
- Do you actually want to be in a ski resort (maximum convenience for the lifts and all the other resort facilities) or would you prefer to be outside (more tranquillity)?

Retirement in the sun

— The Dream —

You're sitting on your terrace enjoying breakfast. There's no need to rush it any more. You're retired, after all. You'll have another cup of coffee in the sunshine and then, what, perhaps a swim in the pool? You feel more cheerful than you have for years. Your doctor never accepted that you suffered from SAD (Seasonal Affective Disorder) but he should see you now, grinning like an idiot even though it's February, one of the worst months back in England. The rheumatism seems to have cleared up, too. And you look younger. Everybody says so (must be the suntan). This afternoon you've got friends coming round for a game of bridge. And this evening the British Club is meeting at the Fábrega bar. Yes, this was the right decision.

— The Reality —

We've a while to go before we get the free bus pass ourselves but plenty of friends in mainland Europe already fit that category. Most of them love life abroad, but that's not to say there aren't problems.

Probably the first thing any retired person thinks about is health. Generally, in EU countries, if you're in receipt of a state pension in the UK you'll be on an equal footing with local retired people. But then, the locals don't always get all their costs met, anyway. And if you've retired early you may not be entitled to free health care at all. Quite a lot of retired people opt for full private health insurance or, at least, a top up.

In 2004 the EU launched a health card scheme to replace the antiquated E111. Belgium, France, Germany, Spain and even Slovenia are enthusiasts, issuing smart cards that entitle their citizens to medical treatment in other EU countries. Britain, as usual, is a laggard. But even so, for the moment, these cards only cover treatment for those who are abroad *temporarily*.

What most Brits do is try to keep a foot in both camps, going back to the UK for treatment when necessary – something that may become more difficult as rules are tightened.

Apart from the cost of health care, there's also the problem of communicating with health professionals. It can be hard enough describing symptoms in your own tongue without the complication of a foreign language. Are your language skills subtle enough to differentiate between the various kinds of pain, or to identify the more remote parts of the body? And even if the medical staff speak English, can you be confident they speak it with the precision necessary for such vital matters? One of our British friends, who has mastered medical jargon in Greek, is kept pretty busy accompanying friends to hospital.

It's true that extra application can make up for the loss of grey cells, but learning a new language definitely gets harder as you get older. (And hospital is only one of the tricky situations where a grasp of language can be vital.) But when you have to stay in hospital language is only the start of your problems. What happens to your other half back at the villa? Can he or she cope all alone? If you were still living in the UK, surrounded by your family, there would be someone to mow the grass, change the light bulbs and cook a meal if necessary. Who's going to take care of that kind of thing now? And, of course, these are the kinds of problems that are going to arise more and more often as you get older. You need someone to help out. Of course, the expat life can be immensely social. If you make friends easily you'll hopefully have neighbours who will step into the breach. But there's nothing like family.

And speaking of family, there's also the patter of tiny feet to consider. You may be delighted at your iron clad excuse for not being able to babysit. You may feel smug that weekends are no longer the time for your house to be methodically taken apart. But you're also probably going to miss making a contribution to your grandchildren's or great grandchildren's development. Women tend to feel this more keenly than men.

One of the real chores of living in a foreign country is the paperwork. You may need a new driving licence. You may need a residence permit. You may need a new will to cover foreign assets. There will be tax forms to fill in. The list goes on and on – with all the atten-

Retirement in the sun

dant standing in queues to see an official who may not understand you anyway. They say you become more patient as you get older. That's good. Because patience is something you're going to need a lot of.

On the other hand, you may be less adaptable than you used to be and more set in your ways. Why can't foreigners do things properly? Fortunately, lots of things have changed in recent years due to technology. Thanks to satellites, you can get some British television almost anywhere. So you don't have to watch 'foreign' television or listen to 'foreign' radio. British newspapers are available year round, not just in summer. Cheap telephone calls are available to and from most places. And cheap flights. British food – even Marmite – is available in the shops wherever British people congregate in significant numbers.

Finally, what happens when one of you dies? What will the other one do? Stay or return to the UK? Inheritance laws can be very different abroad. If you're domiciled in France, for example, all of your estate will be dealt with in accordance with French law. In Spain, on the other hand, you can normally dispose of your assets in accordance with the law in Britain, but even so you should make new wills – one for each country in which you have assets.

If avoiding inheritance tax is an important consideration then take a look at Portugal or Italy. They've abolished the whole damned business (but, unfortunately, not death itself).

— Pros —

○ Moving to southern Europe can be good for many health problems, especially SAD (Seasonal Affective Disorder). New research also

underlines the importance of sunshine for production of vitamin D, essential for the health of skin and bones.
- ☼ Property may be cheaper than in the UK, providing the opportunity to liberate some cash.
- ☼ So many people are retiring to the sun that if you stick with the popular places you'll have no problem making new friends.
- ☼ Moving abroad may be just the stimulation you need to get over the retirement blues.

— Cons —

- ☂ Retirement is already difficult for many people and adding the upheaval of moving to a new country can be too much change too quickly.
- ☂ Moving is stressful at any age and the strain of moving to a new country after retirement can be considerable.
- ☂ Even if the health services are excellent (which they often are) you may not be able to communicate your problems clearly.
- ☂ You'll see less of family left behind in the UK.
- ☂ If you don't already speak the language, retirement age is not the best time to start learning.
- ☂ If you die abroad the inheritance situation can be complicated.
- ☂ If you're a couple then when one of you dies, the other is left to deal with a strange country all alone.

– KEY QUESTIONS –

- Will you go abroad as soon as you retire? Or will you adjust to retirement before moving? Some people find moving is just what they need to give them a new interest – others find the two things coming together are overwhelming.
- Do you know if you're entitled to free health care? Check. If not, can you afford private insurance – or the cost of medical treatment if necessary?
- Can you speak the language well enough to deal with all the problems that crop up when you get older – health care, for example?
- If you're retiring abroad as a couple, what will you do when one of you dies?
- Have you looked into the law on inheritance?
- Would it be a good idea to live within a British community, so you have someone to help you?
- Do you intend to remain abroad until you die, or do you plan to come back 'home' when you feel the end is near?
- Are there cheap flights for you to get back to the UK when necessary, and for relatives to get out to help you?
- Can you really be bothered with all the bureaucratic nonsense at your age?

Romance

— The Dream —

You met on holiday. It wasn't love at first sight. You don't believe in that. But the attraction was strong and you had so much in common. Afterwards, the telephone calls, emails and letters were never ending. You met up twice more and decided to live together. It was agreed you'd be the one to move. Abroad sounded exciting and, anyway, there wasn't a lot to keep you in Britain. Your family were against it but now, a few years on, they've accepted they were wrong. Of course, you have your differences but, if anything, they make the relationship more exciting. You're never bored with one another. And you're still very much in love – with your partner and the country, too.

Romance

— The Reality —

Let's face it. It's hard enough nowadays making any relationship work, without throwing in unnecessary complications. Over four out of every 10 marriages in the UK end in divorce. And the situation for recent marriages is even more disastrous. Now imagine a Brit going abroad to live with someone of a different nationality who speaks a different language and comes from a different culture. Hopeless!

Let's start with language. Modern relationships, if they're to succeed, tend to require an enormous amount of communication. Without wanting to reduce true love to mathematical sounding concepts, the inability to use language with precision is a tremendous hindrance. Even when you both speak the same language fluently it can be difficult enough to understand your partner. Now imagine that you have to converse in pidgin English. 'Me no like it quand tu late home.'

Then there are the cultural problems, especially for British women living with southern European men (most of the time it does seem to be women moving to be with men). Machismo is still alive and well in Mediterranean countries and it doesn't sit well with British feminism.

A young English friend of ours fell in love with a Spaniard whilst she was studying in Barcelona, and after a whirlwind affair she moved in with him. Things soon started to go wrong. Valerie wanted them to do everything together. Jordi, on the other hand, took the view that women are for certain specific things only, all connected with the home. For everything else he preferred to be with his pals. He would go out at night and not return until the early hours, just as when he was living on his own. At the weekends it was even worse. He didn't see it as a problem. Valerie did. The relationship broke up.

In the case of another pan-European couple we know problems didn't emerge until after they'd had children. What had seemed to Fiona such a charming little Provençal village when she first fell in love no longer seemed the right place to bring up youngsters. She wanted them to grow up speaking English as their first language, go to a British school and have British culture. Or, at the very least, be sophisticated residents of the Côte d'Azur, not country bumpkins in the Alpes-Maritimes. Jean-Pierre refused to leave the place he loved to go to the town or, even worse, Britain. And that was the end of that.

And, of course, it's not just a question of your relationship with your partner. It's also a question of your relationship with your partner's family. For example, the French, Spanish, Portuguese, Italians and Greeks all tend to spend summer holidays *en famille*. Which often means in the 'home village'. If you've been used to international travel you might find it all rather dull. At best it might be a beach resort but most likely it will be something primitive in the back of beyond. Once there you might be expected to show a degree of deference not usual in Britain. Even to fall in with the wishes of your partner's father as 'head of the family'. To say nothing of your mother-in-law's intrusive helpfulness. But always remember it could be worse. They might live permanently next door. Or even in the same house.

Then there's the question of not being on an equal footing. You're a stranger in a foreign country with no one to turn to for support.

Romance

Your partner, on the other hand, is on the home pitch with friends and family all around. Let's suppose you disagree about the Mediterranean notion that men are in charge of everything they want to be in charge of and you're in charge of whatever's left. Oh, and that men cannot be expected to do housework. Whenever there are rows – and, believe us, there could be many – it's a long way back home to mum. Meanwhile, *he's* got family and friends close by, all urging him not to give up traditional values for a highfalutin' floozy from the frozen north.

But let's not exaggerate the difficulties. As we've already established (see *Experiencing A Different Way Of Life*) nowhere in Europe is really that different any longer. Nor is learning a foreign language really that hard when you live with a foreign language speaker (see *Becoming Fluent In Another Language*). We know plenty of mixed nationality couples and they're no less happy and no more happy than anybody else. And there are some surprises. We know a British woman who went to live with the youngest of seven brothers on Sardinia. Her parents predicted that moving to such a traditional community would be disaster. But as it turned out, she became the main breadwinner in the relationship while her partner does most of the looking after children. The age difference between her partner and the oldest brother is 18 years and the gulf between the brothers in terms of attitudes is equally wide. If she'd had the misfortune to have fallen in love with the eldest brother things would have been very different. In other words there can be more difference between individuals of a particular nationality – even between brothers – than between nationalities.

And there's one cultural difference that might work in your favour. Divorce in southern Europe is far less common than in Britain. In

Portugal the divorce rate is half the UK figure, in Greece and Spain it's not much over a third and in Italy it's only a quarter. (But if you really want to be sure of staying married go to Japan, where divorce hardly happens at all.) Finally, never go abroad for romance during a recession – statistics show that economic downturns are as bad for relationships as they are for bank balances.

— Pros —

- Love is where you find it.
- If you're really in love there's nothing to discuss.
- Other things are far more significant in a relationship than nationality. For example, statistics from the USA show that smokers are 53 percent more likely to divorce than non-smokers. So give up smoking and go for it.

— Cons —

- Making a success of a relationship is already hard enough without adding language and cultural complications.
- When there's a row you've no one you can turn to for support.
- The break up of a cross-frontier relationship can be extremely complicated.
- If you want to stay in the country after the relationship has ended you may find yourself isolated from former friends and neighbours who are almost bound to side with your ex-partner.

– KEY QUESTIONS –

- Can you communicate sufficiently well with your partner? Are you sure you know enough about him/her and are not merely infatuated with a fiction you yourself have created?
- Is the relationship the only reason for moving? Do you genuinely like the country you're moving to?
- Can you count on any support locally? Can family and friends from the UK easily visit from time to time? Or will you be on your own when there are relationship problems?
- Are you happy that the romance might result in 'foreign' children?
- Have you got a fall back plan if things don't work out?

19

Living among like-minded people

— The Dream —

In Britain you just don't seem to be on the same wavelength. It's almost impossible to find people who think the way you think and who want to do the things you want to do. You need to get yourself to Biarritz where you can make waves with the surf bums. To Empuriabrava to hang out with the freefall adrenaline junkies. To Monaco to monkey around with the deck apes. Or maybe your thing is a bit less physical. The shoppers in Milan. The beautiful people in Gstaad. The nudists at Cap d'Agde. The Eurocrats in Brussels. Gay life in Sitges. Lesbians on Lesbos. Whatever it is you want, mainland Europe's got it and Britain hasn't.

— The Reality —

Certainly there are times all of us want to be surrounded by yes men. And yes women, too. It gets so tiring when people disagree with us. So the idea of living amongst like-minded people can be pretty appealing.

But there's no escaping the fact that you're British. And the inhabitants of the UK are also, mainly, British. So surely you're far more likely to find like-minded people in Britain than anywhere else? London has got to be one of the most diverse cities in the world and Britain one of the countries most tolerant of eccentricity. If you can't find the sort of company you crave in the UK you're not much more likely to find it in Europe. That, anyway, is one of the arguments for staying put.

People who take this view – and there are plenty of them – would point to the unique British sense of humour. That quite distinctive fondness for irony. A love of understatement that isn't normally associated with the Latin temperament (where any opportunity to turn a molehill into a mountain is noisily embraced).

Then there's the British sense of order and fair play. In many parts of Italy, by contrast, the whole idea of queuing is seen as utterly ridiculous. It's not the first come that are first served but those with the sharpest elbows and the loudest voices. And that's another thing: no Latin will ever cross the road to speak to you when a good shout will do just as well.

But this is indulging in stereotypes. And trivia. And, quite obviously, those people who share this particular dream, rightly or wrongly *don't* feel they're in step with the rest of Britain or any part of it.

Kvedja England

You, too, may see yourself as un-British. The problem is, people abroad will probably clock you as accurately as if you were wearing a Union Jack on your head. Yes, it may well be the case that you're a ski nut and want to winter in Chamonix with the other powder hounds. Or that you live, eat and breathe truffles as much as any French *bon vivant*. Or that you're as obsessed with *jai-alai* as a Basque. But that doesn't automatically guarantee you'll be accepted as one of the gang.

There are those little national nuances that are so difficult to conceal. Of course, if you really make an effort you may be able to wean yourself off wearing socks with your sandals. And given copious amounts of factor 1,000 you may be able to stop yourself going bright red in the sun. But will you be able to stop yourself rooting for England when the lads take on your adopted country at footie? The fact is, you're probably never going to be as un-British as you think you are. And certainly not in the eyes of those around you – all the more so if you don't speak the language very well.

We're not saying that because you're a different nationality you can't be fully accepted by a group of people who share the same interests. Daniel Barenboim, for example, has done a marvellous job of bringing young people together across the most ferocious political divide through a shared love of music. And music is only one of the things that can draw people to one another or to a place. We both have a feeling for mountains, pine forests and snow. Where does it come from? We don't know. But it exists and it can't be satisfied in the UK. Other Brits find they're strongly drawn to the dry, aromatic *maquis* of the Mediterranean. Still others (though very few) to the steady rain and moody skies of the Norwegian fjords. But what we *are* observing is that there's an obstacle here to the gratifying sensation

Living amoung like-minded people

of feeling that you're amongst friends with common interests and common emotional responses. The obstacle can be overcome but that's not to say it doesn't exist.

In any event, being like-minded isn't sharing just a single interest in common or agreeing on a few things. It would be extremely difficult to find any two people in the world who didn't agree on anything and who had nothing at all in common. We're surely talking of much more than that. Of hearing a piece of news and *knowing* the reaction of your friends will be exactly the same as your own. Of being able to say what you really think and not be scorned. Of proposing something and feeling confident your friends will want to do it, too.

What it comes down to, then, is that the kind of like-minded people you'll most probably be surrounded by will be other expats. Not necessarily British, but people who have also left their home country and share the same international outlook (or, at the very least, natives of your new country who have travelled a good deal). Who share the same taste for adventure. For change.

In our own experience this tends to be the case. That's not to say we don't have very good friends who are local people. But just as there are little Englanders so there are little Francers and little Espagners and all the rest and it can get tedious to keep hearing that your adopted country is the best in every way – the food is the best food, the music is the best music, the football team is the best football team, and so on. Especially if you left Britain because you got fed up with that kind of attitude there.

So don't count on being 'accepted' however much you crave it. And don't be upset if you're not. Country folk don't even accept their fellow nationals from the towns. In Spain, for example, people from Barcelona are known in the countryside as *quemachos* (pronounced chemichos), because the first thing they say when they arrive is *Que macho!* Meaning: How beautiful! So what chance do you have? It's just normal human behaviour. Be prepared for it. Accept it philosophically. Don't hold it against anybody. And you'll have a better time than if you set too much store on finding people who think like you in every way.

— Pros —

- With 450 million people in Europe as opposed to just under 60 million in the UK you must stand a better chance of finding what you seek.
- There are hobbies, activities and lifestyles on mainland Europe that, for geographical reasons, just don't exist in the UK.
- If it's an international outlook that appeals to you then, yes, you'll find plenty of like-minded expats from Britain and other north European countries settled elsewhere.

— Cons —

- Britain has some of the world's most cosmopolitan cities — you're far more likely to find the kind of urban people you like there than in a city abroad. As for the countryside, you're never going to be accepted as a son or daughter of a village abroad — you'd better get used to the idea.
- It could get rather dull being surrounded by yes men and yes women.
- When it comes to finding people who share your views and tastes a chat room in cyberspace might be a better and easier bet than Eurospace.

Living amoung like-minded people

- If you can't speak the language very well you're never going to reach an intimate understanding of other people, whether you're like-minded or not.

— KEY QUESTIONS —

- Have you ever analysed why you feel you're a square peg in a round, British hole? It may be important to finding a solution.
- However much you may fit into a clique abroad you'll always remain an outsider in the country. Are you prepared for that?
- Are you willing to make the effort to speak the language like a native? If not, like-mindedness may remain elusive.
- What aspects of your chosen destination make you sure you'll be with like-minded people? Now list all the things you don't agree with. Which list is longest?

Foodie heaven

— The Dream —

First thing in the morning you'll nip down to the local bakery for too-hot-to-touch crusty bread and a bag of plump, buttery croissants. (You made the jam from given away plums last week.) When you get back you'll grind the coffee beans and eat breakfast *al fresco*. Later, with the big basket resting on your hip, you'll stock up with fresh vegetables from the garden of the old chap down the road and with fish, still gasping, bought for half a sixpence from the weathered fishermen on the quay. Once a week there'll be the visit to the market — shining piles of tomatoes, aubergines, red peppers, courgettes, melons and sun touched local oranges. As pure and wholesome as you feel after eating them. Then there are the restaurants. You'll adventure endlessly into 'discoveries' known only to a select few, where the owner will recognise you, greet you with a cheery *bon appétit* and lead you to your favourite table.

Foodie heaven

— The Reality —

There's a reason you ate convenience foods in Britain. Yes, convenience! All this real, local produce sounds wonderful until you have onions to peel, the knobbly bits on the Jerusalem artichokes to wash and the green beans to de-string. And don't forget the bloody washing up. It's enough to drive you to another glass of the local red.

And there's another downside to the Continental preference for fresh, local food. You won't very easily find the ingredients for the Indian curry you used to enjoy on a Saturday night, nor any of that Australian wine to wash it down. If you want choice, stay in Britain.

And even the range of local products isn't as extensive as it used to be. You can thank the EU for protecting you from food poisoning, or blame it, according to your point of view. Years ago we used to buy goat's cheese from a little farm high up in the Pyrenees. The fresh medallions were as light as champagne while the mature, slightly shrunken roundels were as tangy as old parmesan. But it's not possible any more — the facilities just didn't measure up to the new EU norms. Pity!

That having been said, if you're dogged enough there's always somebody who knows somebody whose brother has an illicit goat in the back garden. They can't stop you risking salmonella if you really insist. Nor, come to that, blindness. Our good friend Pepe makes his own *orujo* distilled from the left over seeds and skins from the year's wine pressings. It's powerful stuff. Totally disinfecting we always think, thankfully, as a crowd of us all sample the latest product from a single, unwashed glass.

There are two audiences that probably won't appreciate any of your efforts anyway. Your local friends. And your children (if you have any). Sebastian, a Spanish pal of ours, always brings at least some food with him dressed up in the guise of a present. The real reason, of course, is that he doesn't trust our cooking.

As for children they are, of course, notorious for saying "Urrgh!" to anything that tastes the slightest bit different. Scientists postulate it's a mechanism, left over from a few hundred thousand years ago, to prevent infants poisoning themselves as they crawled around the cave and its environs. Maybe, but it's pretty exasperating all the same. So while you're slaving over *poussins citronés aux fines herbes* they'll be whining to go to McDonald's. Which is where all their local friends will already be.

Yes, the 'oldies' may be sticking to real food but the younger generation is much more likely to opt for the fast food you thought you'd left behind. Which doesn't bode well for the future. They said the French would never tolerate the sacrilege of McDonald's. They said the French like to take time over a meal. They said the French recall their lives as a series of great meals punctuated by inconsequentialities. 'They' were wrong. McDonald's is big in France. And they didn't have to change anything. The Big Macs and Potatoes De Luxe are the same as McDonald's everywhere. Only the style of the customers is a little different. Standing behind a French youngster in the queue recently, we heard a description of a new dish, something to do with chicken in a bun, which sounded more Egon Ronay. 'Délicieuse!' the young gourmet was insisting to her friend. 'La sauce, mmmnn, c'est vraiment extra.'

Even if you hold out against McDonald's the family run local shop can still torpedo your efforts. There your children will learn to say

Foodie heaven

(in French or Greek or whatever) words like crisps, chocolate, lolly and large packet. The cat sleeping comfortably on the bags of macaroni has a certain rustic charm but, somehow, it never seems quite so enchanting when Minou is lying on the meat counter. So, deeply ungrateful for your children's language class, you're quite soon deserting the shop for the big supermarket. The supermarket is so clean, so cheap and, with no need to speak to anybody, so well adapted to self-deception. You can lay your bunch of celery, a bag of tomatoes, a couple of lettuces and six litres of mineral water over the top of all those ready made hamburger meals, deep frozen French fries and 6-packs, and steer towards the checkout muttering about "this wonderful Mediterranean diet". Why, you'll almost believe it yourself. But your trousers won't do up any easier and the scales will know the truth.

As for restaurants, most people would say the French have the best cuisine in Europe and we'd tend to agree. It's in the DNA. If you want to wind up a French person just say you can't tell the difference between Burgundy and Bordeaux. Or between margarine and butter. But you have to accept that in France you get French food and French wine prepared the French way. That's to say, when you order trout, that's exactly what you get. Nothing less, nothing more – except a dob of sauce and a sprig of parsley. You'll come out of plenty of the more 'sophisticated' restaurants a lot poorer and still hungry. Great if all this is what you want. Irritating otherwise.

— Pros —

○ There may be the same bad food temptations in your new life as in the old but a healthy Mediterranean diet is more readily available in Provence than in Peterborough and you'll be surrounded by people

Di Widzenia Anglia

who treat it as their daily bread. Talking of bread, try eating fresh bread rubbed with garlic, smeared with olive oil and flavoured with the addition of a ripe, juicy, giant summer tomato. Garlicky breath? When in Catalonia smell like a Catalan.

- Despite the European 'norms' there are still many more local producers (from whom you can buy direct) in countries like France and Italy than there are in Britain.
- Booze is generally less expensive than back home and the measures much, much more generous.
- Let's face it, the standard of cuisine is just vastly higher in France than in Britain. If you're a genuine foodie you're going to be surrounded by people who speak your language – Aaah! Mmmm! and so forth.

– Cons –

- You may love drowning everything in olive oil and trying new things like goat's cheese, octopus and snails, but your children will hate 'foreign muck'.
- Even Continental food is changing – for the worst. Chilling, flash freezing, ready made meals, microwaves and things done 'fast' are all beginning to make their presence felt.
- If you live in a tourist area, be prepared for restaurant prices to go up and standards to fall during the season.
- You just won't find the same variety of international ingredients in Continental supermarkets (especially French ones) as you do in Britain.

– KEY QUESTIONS –

- Are you adventurous with your food or would you rather stick with the jam butties you know?
- If you've got children with you will they co-operate in being adventurous with food?
- Have you got the budget to enjoy all this wonderful food?
- Until you've mastered the language, are you going to risk misunderstandings by shopping in places where you have to ask for things?
- Having suffered a misunderstanding (as in above) are you big enough to get on and fry/broil/bake aforementioned unexpected ingredient?
- Are you able to organise a system (e.g. friends visiting) for obtaining supplies of the quintessentially British things you still crave (such as Marmite and steak and kidney pudding)?
- Are you prepared to put up with rebellious bodily functions until you're accustomed to the change in diet?

# Becoming a real European

— The Dream —

Your father fought in the Second World War. Your grandfather fought in the First World War. A Europe in which there will never again be a war is an ideal worth supporting. So is the concept of a Europe which stretches from the Mediterranean to beyond the Arctic Circle, and from the Atlantic to the Aegean. A Europe of 450 million people. A Europe with a single currency. A Europe you can move around in as freely as in the country you were born. A Europe with a world voice. And you don't want to be on the periphery, either physically or politically. You don't want to live in a country that's Europhobic or, at best, Eurosceptic. You want to be right in there, in the middle of it all. It's a heady brew.

— The Reality —

So are mainland Europeans really more, well, *European*? In fact, yes. There are plenty of surveys to show that Continentals are far more enthusiastic about the EU than the Brits.

In Luxembourg, for example, it's difficult to find anybody who *doesn't* support the euro. The Greeks, the Italians, the Belgians, the Dutch and the Spanish are crazy about it. In fact, on mainland Europe only in Finland and Denmark will you find less than majority support. Compare that with the UK where only about a quarter of the population care to abandon the pound. Or take the EU constitution. Even the Swedes who are, to say the least, suspicious of the euro are convinced of its importance.

Of course, opinions are changing all the time and you'll always hear complaints as you travel around the Continent. Moaning about the EU is a hobby and, when it suits them, national governments are very happy to encourage it. When things go right they take the credit, when things go wrong they blame the EU. Plenty of people will tell you that prices have gone up as a direct result of the euro. But then they shrug and grin. Because who wants to have to change currency every time they cross a frontier — and lose a percentage of their money each time?

This is something Continentals do quite a lot, you see. In Britain going abroad is a *big thing*. Passport. Travel insurance. Money belts. Insect repellent. Plug adapters. Toilet rolls. Meanwhile people from Luxembourg slip across the frontier to go shopping in Belgium or Germany or France with no more preparation than the average Brit would make for an expedition to Tesco. Austrians have the choice of

Na Shledanou Anglie

seven neighbouring countries to find something a little more exotic for dinner – Germany, Switzerland, Italy, Slovenia, Hungary, Slovakia and the Czech Republic.

Where we live in Spain we can tootle over to France in about 20 minutes and often do. There's something rather exhilarating about living near a frontier and yet being able to cross it without hindrance. And to many Europeans it's just an everyday sort of thing. They eat breakfast in one country, work in another and make love in a third. Being on an island makes people insular; being on the mainland makes people open.

Quite apart from all these day trips, European populations are getting pretty mixed up permanently, especially around the Mediterranean. All that blue stuff acts like blotting paper for pasty faced northerners. In nine out of the 15 Spanish coastal areas, for example, foreign owned properties are in the majority. We lived in a village in France where there were people from Spain, Italy, Holland, Germany and Belgium. Oh, and of course, France. Here, in our part of Spain, you can throw in North Africans and South Americans, too.

But it would be wrong to paint a picture of rosy, good natured togetherness without noting that some people seem to be moving in the opposite direction. Everywhere groups of people are claiming characteristics that mark them out as special. There it's the Corsicans, over there the Cornish, and here it's the Catalans who distinguish themselves from the non-Catalan Spanish by putting Catalan donkey stickers on their cars (as opposed to the Spanish bull).

Occasionally this can work in favour of Europe. Plenty of Catalans

Becoming a real European

will say they're Catalan first, European second and Spanish third. The idea of being part of Europe reinforces their sense of identity. What works against Europe is the notion that nationality defines identity and that Europe erases it. There are plenty of people who, although living abroad, nevertheless want to stick with their 'own kind'. It makes you wonder why they moved at all.

Unfortunately there are enough people who insist on the importance of nationality to cause problems. You can see it right now in places like Mallorca where the locals complain of being overrun by foreigners. They don't like going into a supermarket and finding that the staff only speak a foreign language. Meanwhile, the expats insist on their right to live as they did in their own country. None of it is a recipe for trouble free integration. And anti-European sentiment is growing in many quarters, rather than diminishing. Some commentators blame it all on Britain for having started Europhobia with its negative attitudes.

Can there, then, be such a thing as a European culture? We've been arguing pretty hard throughout the book that, when it comes down to fundamentals, people all over Europe are just the same as one another and as Brits. And they are. But, on the other hand, yes, there are those subtle little things which denote a Continental European. There's the taste for those kinds of films where people endlessly stir cups of coffee and nothing much else ever happens. The delight in sitting outside cafés rather than inside. An ability to drink alcohol without having to trash the town centre. A tendency, on entering a shop, to wish everyone good day. A penchant for men to kiss one another. The routine ability to speak from two to five languages (out of the 20 that are 'official' in the EU). A general feeling that people

Na Shledanou Anglie

in other parts of the world should be able to get on with their lives without being told what to do by Westerners.

But, admittedly, none of this is the same as boldly proclaiming: "I'm a European". Are there really, in fact, any Europeans to join? Are there people who would like to see the words *European Union* writ large on their passports? Or even *United States of Europe*? Well, there are certainly some. But they're in a minority at the moment.

And there's always the danger that Europe will become America. Jeans, hamburgers and baseball caps are everywhere. And Tom Cruise is just as popular as Penelope Cruz. More and more, European culture is just own brand Cola to America's Coca-Cola.

Which way will it all go? Will the EU become a political reality that can balance the power of the USA? Or is the European dream over before it ever really got going? Perhaps the most significant finding among all the polls is this from Gallup: EU residents trust the EU more than they do their own governments.

— Pros —

- As an English speaker you're already fluent in the *de facto* language of all Europe.
- Living on mainland Europe you can visit other EU countries without having to get in an aeroplane, a boat or a tunnel, or change currency.
- You'll have much more the sense of being in a 'United States of Europe' with a far larger population than the United States of America.

Becoming a real European

— Cons —

- With 20 'official' languages spoken in the EU, to say nothing of all the others, you're just never going to be able to feel part of a truly homogenous entity.
- There's anti-European feeling on the mainland, even if it's less than in the UK, and it seems to be growing rather than diminishing.
- Given time, the 'United States of Europe' might not be much different from the United States of America.

— KEY QUESTIONS —

- If you're an enthusiast for Europe have you considered that you could have more impact by staying in Britain and campaigning?
- The place you're going may be on mainland Europe but are you sure it's Europhile rather than Europhobic?
- Is there a happy mix of nationalities or are there tensions? Mallorcans, for example, are getting pretty fed up with the huge number of foreign residents.
- Would you really be happy to have the words *United States of Europe* on your passport? Or would you always think of the UK as 'home'?

22

Becoming an artist or writer

— The Dream —

It worked for Hemingway. It worked for F Scott Fitzgerald. It worked for James Joyce. You get away from your own country and look back on it with a clearer perspective. Or you're stimulated by new and exciting experiences — you find your subject. Or you move into a provocative, artistic milieu where artists, writers and philosophers have gathered to forge a new artistic direction. Think of the Fauves at Collioure. Think of Dalí and Bunuel and Lorca at Cadaqués. If only, if only, you could get away from dreary old Britain with its old fashioned ideas, its dull predictability and its Artistic Establishment holding you back then you would stand a chance of making it.

Becoming an artist or writer

– The Reality –

Yes, it works for some people. But it doesn't work for most.

Let's face the facts. If moving abroad automatically made you a great artist then there'd be hundreds of thousands in Spain right now.

The really awful thing is you used to kid yourself and everybody else you hadn't made it as a creative force because you didn't have either the time or the right environment to work in. Now you suddenly have to face up to the possibility it could actually be lack of talent. You have the time. You have the environment. And still you can't get anywhere.

And why should you? Abroad is the last place to go if you want to make a success of your talents. In the first place, you can't promote yourself, you can't do any public relations and you can't network any longer. All the agents are back in London. All the editors. All the art directors. All the publishers. All the important galleries. At least you had a few contacts when you lived in the UK but now they've all forgotten you. In fact, isn't London precisely one of the places a creative person would head for, if they had any sense? Hasn't London been good enough for David Bailey? And Francis Bacon? And Tracey Emin? And Damien Hirst?

Far from producing 'serious work' you're much more likely to end up churning out rubbish for the tourist trade – paintings of sunsets in gaudy colours, pots in the shape of penises (yes, it really happens in the Spanish resort of Peniscola), photographs of topless girls or hunky men for postcards (you should be so lucky) or writing guidebooks to the 101 different goat cheeses to be found in the area.

What you need most of all as a creative person is time. You need the time to write your novel, paint your paintings or compose your symphony, which means having enough money not to have to work at anything else. But there's no automatic reason why moving abroad will provide that. Of course, if you sell a very expensive house in London and buy a very cheap house in the Peloponnese then the spare cash could provide the buffer you need. But, equally, you could liberate capital by moving to a cheap part of the UK. (And, of course, you have to be willing to take the financial risk of whether your work will eventually sell and repay the investment.)

The very act of moving abroad eats time. Even when you've settled in there'll still be the extension to build, the studio to organise and the garden to get straight. Apart from that, time is anyway a commodity in short supply in expatland. For a start there are all kinds of seductive distractions. Presumably they formed part of the motivation for the move in the first place. It's very hard, for example, to keep typing or sculpting when it's sunny and you know there are going to be gorgeous bodies on the beach. Or if you know there's new powder on the *piste*. There are only two answers to this. One is to incorporate these pleasures into your work (e.g. write about skiing, paint people on the beach). The other is a large dose of self-discipline. (Boring!)

What's more, quite a lot of expats have literally nothing to do. If you work at home they'll assume you don't really have anything to do either and may drop by for a chat. It's very hard to convince them that while, yes, you may well have been on the terrace when they arrived, you were actually *thinking* and cannot be disturbed.

Yet another problem is that while your creative juices may have been

Becoming an artist or writer

stimulated by your new surroundings your target audience back in the UK won't know what you're on about. To you, the local fish market may have become intensely fascinating. But back in Newcastle or Wales it will mean almost nothing. Even worse, you may be so contented with the move your creative juice gland actually dries up.

All that having been said, expat life has become easier than ever before for the creative person. For example, you can now email drafts, finished articles, photographs and other images back to the UK. You can do your research on the internet rather than at the British Library. And when you do need to return to the UK for meetings then – provided you're living in a suitable area – you can nip back courtesy of one of the no-frills airlines. Finally, being a penniless bohemian in the Med is nothing like being a penniless bohemian in Paris. In your northern city garret you may be forced to burn your manuscripts or paintings to get through the winter. That won't happen in southern Europe. And, nowadays, no poverty stricken artist in Europe is ever left to die of starvation.

– Pros –

- A new environment can be stimulating or give you a new perspective on your old environment.
- For certain kinds of work being abroad may be the only option – for example, to write a travel book or paint mountains.
- If you move somewhere idyllic – and have space for guests – you may be able to entice art patrons, agents and the like out to visit you.
- The internet has made the expat artist's life easier than ever before.

— Cons —

- Unless you're producing work to sell in the local area you'll find the lack of contact with London agents and galleries a serious hurdle to selling anything.
- The amount you spend on communication (telephone and travel) may leap, especially if you need to return to the UK at frequent intervals.
- People who commission work tend to favour artists, writers and composers they're in personal touch with. It may be a case of out of sight, out of mind.
- You'll be in local competition with the thousands of other arty types who have already made the move.
- If suffering is essential to creativity moving to the Med could be a retrograde step.

Becoming an artist or writer

– KEY QUESTIONS –

- Are you sure being in some other place (abroad) is essential to your creativity?
- Have you actually got any firm evidence, anyway, that you're not merely creative but also commercial? Is this more a fantasy than a dream?
- Do you need to share the stimulating company of other creative people or do you prefer to work in splendid isolation? Near us, at Cadaqués, artists are as common as fishermen (more common, probably, given the state of the fish catch). And every third expat is either a photographer, a painter or a writer. But there are other places you'll be completely on your own.
- How are you going to market your work? Will you have to keep going back to London? How much is that going to cost? Can you develop new markets abroad?
- How are you going to support yourself (and dependents) while you're waiting for the world to recognise your talents? Is your partner really *that* tolerant?

Living in the wilderness

— The Dream —

There's not a sound. Nothing, that is, other than the gurgling of the stream, the calls of the bee eaters and the breeze rustling the leaves. From your house you can see in every direction. And in every direction it's the same thing. Nothing. Just evergreen oaks, a few pine trees, rocks, cliffs, aromatic scrub. The silhouette of a buzzard. No other houses. No surfaced roads. No neighbours from hell. And at night, without a street light to be seen, it's a paradise of stars. It seems you could reach up and touch the Milky Way. As soon as you arrived you felt the stress ebbing away. Now you wouldn't want to live in any other fashion. It's so romantic. So earthy. So in touch with everything that matters. So holistic.

Living in the wilderness

— The Reality —

We wouldn't actually say we live in the wilderness, but quite a lot of people who visit us think we do. We have solar panels for electricity and a well for water. Of course, it depends what you call wilderness. When we bought our ruin it was reached by a couple of kilometres of dirt track from the nearest village. That was then. Now a surfaced road passes nearby, thanks to EU funding for upgrading the infrastructure of member states. This is one of the realities, you see – wilderness is everywhere under threat from so called 'improvement'.

Let's face it. There really isn't very much real wilderness left in Europe and a downside of the EU is that what remains is disappearing faster than it would have done.

If you want real wilderness you have to think of countries like Argentina and New Zealand (on average, only about a dozen or so people per square kilometre) or Canada and Australia (around three people per square kilometre). That is, places far away. Or totally inhospitable to man and woman. Like Greenland, for example. Now you're really talking. Greenlanders get about 35 square kilometres *each*. (By comparison, every square kilometre of the UK contains an average of 239 people.)

In Europe the best you can do is Sweden at a little over 20 people per square kilometre, Finland at 16 or Norway (not in the EU) at 14. But Scandinavia is cold. And dark all winter. Could you really face that without going mad?

It's not so much that finding wilderness is a problem, even with six billion people on the planet. No, the real trick is to find wilderness where it's *nice* to live. The sort of wilderness where it's sunny but never too hot (or cold) with green wild flower meadows and ancient woodlands and, ideally, with a mountain sloping down to a secluded little bay. When you find that, let us know and we'll be right over.

Even supposing you *do* find some wilderness to your taste, it won't be easy to get permission to live there. Which is one reason why there's still some wilderness left. You wouldn't want it any other way. Nobody should be allowed to live in the wilderness. Except, of course, *you*. Your best bet is to take up farming. Farmers can get permission when nobody else can.

But let's suppose you have found some wilderness and that you've got permission to live there. What's it like?

The nearest we've come ourselves is a barn we bought at around 1,400 metres in the Pyrenees, 20 minutes on foot from a forestry track in summer, one hour on snowshoes from the valley bottom in winter. We took our water from a stream, cooked on a fire and brought our provisions in on horseback. It felt authentic. But the *mairie* wanted us out for breaching regulations and, anyway, there was no way of earning a living. Fairly soon we had to give up.

But we made friends with a family in a similar barn across the far side of the valley who showed considerably more tenacity. There had been periodic attempts to evict them for not having planning permission, but they always foundered on the opposing laws that protect people from homelessness. Our friends have now lived there about 20 years without any 'modern conveniences'. Their salads are literally handfuls of whatever happens to be growing nearby at the time. The oil lamps give a wonderful, romantic glow at night, but have you ever tried reading by one?

Probably the only practical way to live in real wilderness in Europe

Living in the wilderness

is to run a refuge. Like that you can get to live in some pretty spectacular places. The problem is, you have to share your home with dozens – sometimes hundreds – of other people. Probably not what you came to the wilderness for.

In reality you're going to have to compromise on semi-wilderness. Which is what we've done.

To find water we had a diviner. He put his hand up in the air in a kind of Fascist salute and marched around until he had settled on an area. Then, for more precision, he switched to a pendulum. Once he had decided on the exact spot he 'weighed' pebbles in the palm of his hand to determine the depth. We didn't believe any of it but it was great fun. The contractors set up something like a miniature oil well and set to work. By lunchtime the spoil was coming up moist and by mid-afternoon we struck water at 64 metres, just as the diviner had said. Impressive? Maybe. But, then, as a geologist friend pointed out later, there's water everywhere at a certain level. It's called the water table. Maybe it was magic, maybe it was just common sense married to a little knowledge of geology. The important thing is, we had water.

Electricity was another problem. At two and a half kilometres from the nearest pylon, the only option was solar power. Not cheap. The whole set-up cost about as much as a decent family saloon. The good news is that we don't have electricity bills. The bad news is that the batteries and the panels only last a dozen years or so, which works out at over £1,000 a year. And we don't get very much electricity for that – not more than about 4kw a day. And none at all when there's a succession of cloudy days. Hallo generator, goodbye tranquillity.

The entire house, being open plan, is heated by two wood burning stoves. They keep us pretty busy all year cutting dead trees and

Zbogom angleški

chopping wood and when the weather is really cold there's a constant procession keeping them fed.

Communications are the other problem. Technology provided us with a telephone via a radio link and recently that's been upgraded to cellular technology. But the postman doesn't call – we have to collect our mail from a box two kilometres away – and there's zero chance of urgent packages being delivered.

Life in the wilderness is *hard* and even in the semi-wilderness it's still pretty demanding. As long as you understand that, and are sure that's what you want, fine. Felling trees. Chopping wood. Clearing land for the vegetable garden. Doing all the maintenance yourself.

And going out at night can become a major event when you have to negotiate a flooded track without lighting to get home again. Things that used to be so quick and easy become major problems. If you're really in the wilderness it isn't going to be easy getting the plumber.

– Pros –

- As much peace and quiet as you can stand.
- No neighbours to fall out with.
- Nobody to bother you.
- You can live exactly as you please.
- Plenty of natural exercise.
- The spiritual side of life comes with the territory.

– Cons –

- It's a hard life.
- 'Normal' things like shopping, going to the cinema or to restaurants become major logistical exercises.

Living in the wilderness

- When things go wrong you have to be self-reliant – it won't be easy getting a plumber or an electrician.
- You'll be cut off from other people.
- Wilderness living can actually be damned expensive. A useful solar electric system, for example, costs as much as a good family saloon.
- Unless you're going to live in an incredibly basic way, wilderness homes tend to require a lot of maintenance – the solar power system, the wind generator, the septic tank, the reed bed, the well...
- The wilderness tends to be a place of extremes. Rain funnels into gullies and becomes a raging torrent, insects appear in Biblical numbers and forest fires threaten total destruction.

– KEY QUESTIONS –

- Exactly how much wilderness do you really want? Do you really mean wilderness or do you mean the *countryside* with no neighbours closer than half a kilometre?
- Are you self-reliant? Will you be able to deal with all the maintenance problems with the wind generator, the solar panels and the septic tank?
- Are you fit enough to cope with all the wilderness jobs like chopping the wood, clearing the ground and maintaining the access?
- How will you earn a living? If we're talking real wilderness it's going to take a long time to get to the office. If you intend to live off the land then are you prepared to be poor?
- Are you sure you can adjust to the lower standard of living the wilderness guarantees?

24

Having your own olive grove

— The Dream —

Friends have come for dinner. The table is on the terrace, illuminated by candles. The cicadas are creaking in the background. You unveil your first dish of feta cubes marinated in olive oil. Your guests exclaim. Such delicious olive oil! So buttery! So smooth! And isn't there, don't you think, just a hint of pepper about it? Why, you can't get anything like this in the supermarket in England. You permit a knowing, slightly superior, smile to play at the corners of your mouth. Well, yes, you murmur, actually this is oil from our own olive trees. At least 100 years old, you know. Quite beautiful and truly mystical. The oil is stone pressed, in fact. And, of course, totally organic.

— The Reality —

Believe us, once you've had your own olive trees you'll never again complain about the price of olive oil. It's *cheap* compared with all the work involved.

Let's deal straight away with most people's first question. Black olives are simply green olives that have been left on the tree longer. So that sorts that out.

The olive year begins with pruning. The basic theory is that too many branches result in numerous, tiny olives whereas you want big, juicy olives which are full of oil. Different areas have different styles but the essential is a tree that is open in the middle and whose branches droop outwards for easy picking. Apart from anything else, the way you maintain your olive grove will affect your standing with the locals, in the same way your car might have done back in England. A well pruned, orderly grove will gain you respect.

Weeding is the next big chore. You need to keep the ground clear for picking (see below) and to reduce the risk that fire might damage the trees. Fire is an ever present threat. Most growers use weedkiller to keep the area between the trees free of grass and plants. But if you're an organic purist you may question this and go for mowing or hand weeding. While you're at it, you may want to sprinkle fertiliser.

By midsummer you'll need to protect your trees from pests. If you don't spray, you'll end up with maggots in a high proportion of olives. That's not too serious if you're only going to make oil but is pretty unattractive if you actually want olives to eat.

Harvesting is done between October and February, depending on climate and whether you want green or black olives.

If you want green olives for eating, the timing is fairly critical. When you stick your thumbnail into the olive it should feel juicy but still crisp. There should be a definite noise as the nail penetrates. A sort of *schkriss*. By the way, don't lick your fingers or try eating any olives off the tree. The taste is so unbelievably bitter the sour flavour will linger in the mouth for hours. How, you will wonder, did anyone ever imagine that olives could be made edible? It's a mystery.

On the other hand, if you want to eat black olives, or to have oil, timing is a little less critical. Olives picked earlier tend to have a more delicate flavour while those picked later will contain more oil and have a stronger flavour. But leave the olives too long and the oil will be unpalatable. Also, the longer they're on the tree the more you risk the whole crop being taken by starlings. Literally thousands can descend on a grove and strip it in a day. It happened to our friend Carlos.

There are several ways of picking olives and none of them is easy. The best is to pick them by hand, one at a time. For that, it helps to have absolutely nothing else to do in your life. Somewhat faster is to lay netting round the tree and either comb it with a sort of rake or beat it with a stick to make the olives fall off. Where we live, farmers wait for the *tramuntana* – the fierce wind from the mountains – to blast the olives off. Then they collect them from the ground with a machine a bit like a spiky lawn roller (hence the need for the ground to be clear of weeds). But the resulting damage means lower quality oil, especially if the olives are left lying on the ground for very long. A friend of ours waited a week after the *tramuntana* and the

Having your own olive grove

result was an oil that could only be used for treating wood – brought the grain out a treat.

Basically, you really have to love the whole business of olives otherwise it's horribly boring. It helps to throw a barbecue on harvest day so all your friends will come to help – you may have to bribe them with some oil, too. Surely there must be an easier way? Well, there is a system of shaking the tree but you need an expensively equipped tractor for that and it only works with young specimens of varieties developed for the purpose – you can't very easily shake a 500 year old tree with limbs the size of footballers' thighs.

If you want to eat your olives you have to do something to get rid of the appalling taste. The standard method is to leach the bitterness out by soaking in frequent changes of water, a process that takes about three months. Most people can't be bothered to wait that long so accelerate the whole business with a solution of caustic soda. It doesn't sound very organic but it works and it doesn't harm the flavour…much.

If you want oil, on the other hand, that's not something you can do at home. There is a method of squeezing the olives in the folds of a cloth, like wringing out the washing, but you'll be dead before you get a decent quantity of oil that way. You need to find a mill. If you only have a small quantity the usual system is that you bring your olives and are given a proportionate amount of oil in return. The obvious problem with this is *the oil will not be from your own olives*. For that, you need an old fashioned press that operates with small quantities. Where we live we can take our olives to the old mill at Roses and watch them being crushed by the stone wheel before being squeezed between mats

Tot siens Engeland

of esparto fibre. It's fascinating to see and exciting to taste the first of the oil.

A typical tree yields between 15kg and 30kg of olives and the conversion could be as low as 7 percent or as high as 20 percent – that's to say, 100kg of olives produce between seven and 20 litres of oil. At the end of the day, from a grove of 20 trees, you might end up with from 20 litres to 120 litres of oil – it all depends on location, climate, age of tree, variety, the moment of harvesting and the pressing system used.

It quite often happens that an olive grove is abandoned, usually because the owner is too old to work it and none of the relatives can be bothered. So if you don't own an olive grove you might be able to borrow someone else's. That's what we did the first year. The agreement was that we'd do the work and the oil would be split 50-50. What we hadn't taken into account was the tools we'd have to buy – pruning saws, secateurs, ladder, spray for herbicide, fertiliser… It all cost far more than the oil was worth, especially when our time was taken into account. And yet, when we had the chance to buy a grove we jumped at it. Which just about sums up the whole mystery of olives.

— Pros —

- Old olive trees have a magic that links you with the past.
- Olive trees are beautiful.
- Olive groves are a good investment.
- Oil from your own grove will have a distinctive flavour – the oil you buy in the supermarket is always a blend.
- If you have your own trees you know the oil is produced the way you want it.

Having your own olive grove

– Cons –

- Olive groves are a lot of work for a very small return.
- It's actually cheaper – and much easier – to buy olive oil than to produce it on a small scale.

– KEY QUESTIONS –

- Having an olive grove sounds very romantic, but are you really prepared for all the hard work?
- If you don't have the time or inclination for manual labour, do you know somebody who can manage the grove for you (usually in return for 50 percent to 60 percent of the harvest)?
- Do you just want enough olives and olive oil for your own use or do you expect to make money from your olive grove? If so, how will you sell your olives and your oil? Can you join a co-operative? Making money growing olives isn't easy except on a big scale.

What people say about living abroad

Before we began writing this book we ran a survey to find out what dreams people had about living abroad and how those compared with the reality. The topics we've covered in this book have been selected on the basis of responses to the questionnaire.

Whom did we survey?

We surveyed just over 100 expats living in nearly 10 countries. Almost half of these were in Spain and a fifth in France, a reflection of the popularity of those two countries among British expats in Europe. But we also had responses from expats in Italy (10 percent), Greece (6 percent) and Portugal (6 percent) with a handful from other countries.

Some of these were contacts we had made living in France or Spain or while travelling (or friends and acquaintances of theirs). Others were members of expat societies or of expat chat groups on the web. We didn't ask people to give their age on the questionnaire, but the youngest we know of was 20 and the oldest 77.

What people say about living abroad

Interestingly, the pattern that was established by the first 20 questionnaires was continued by all the later questionnaires that were returned. It seems, therefore, that a larger sample would be unlikely to alter the main findings in any way.

It's fair to say that our survey didn't include any previous expats who have returned to their homeland. Perhaps if we'd been able to track them down in sufficient numbers to conduct a representative survey they would have been slightly less positive about the experience. However our experience suggests that while some people do return because the move doesn't work out for them, many more return for practical reasons, from work to elderly parents who need looking after. In any case, as we've said all along, we believe that if you take on board the advice in this book, the move abroad will be successful for you whether it turns out to be permanent or not.

We consider the results are as unbiased and representative as possible for the countries surveyed and the questions put. If we'd asked people who went to live in Iceland they would probably have given rather different responses to the ones we got from people living in Spain. But we wanted to concentrate on the most popular destinations.

Country	% of respondents
Spain	47
France	19
Italy	10
Portugal	6
Greece	6
Other	12

Au Revoir Angleterre

So what were people's favourite dreams?

We listed 34 dreams about living abroad, based on our own experiences and of talking to other expats we know. We then asked respondents to tick the four that most applied to them. We also left a space for respondents to describe any dream of theirs that hadn't been included on our list. From this we took the 24 most popular dreams.

One of the most interesting findings is that people dream of moving abroad for fairly general reasons rather than to achieve something specific. Almost nobody, for example, ticked *Having A Boat In The Med* or *Year Round Gardening* while *Having Your Own Vineyard* got zero votes. It was all much more to do with the big picture.

Enjoying A Better Climate was a huge motivation, chosen by almost half of all respondents. Obviously this is pretty specific to Brits moving to southern Europe. Not surprisingly, none of the respondents who had moved from Britain to Denmark ticked this dream. In other words, it's not a universal dream for people moving abroad but it is overwhelmingly important for most Brits who move to the Med.

An interesting point is that despite this emphasis on the weather, only 11 percent ticked *Being Near Sunny Beaches*. Maybe it seemed too frivolous a reason or, more likely, most respondents' enjoyment of a better climate is more to do with the general sense of well being.

Next most important dream was *Experiencing A Different Way Of Life* (37 percent). Nobody we followed up with had anything very specific in mind. It doesn't seem to be to do with dreaming of, say, late night barbecues on the beach, or wearing exotic clothes. It was much more the vague notion that there must be more things in life

What people say about living abroad

than can be found in Nuneaton.

Third in importance was *Life Will Somehow Be Better* (32 percent). This seems to reflect the almost universal human belief that doing something relatively dramatic like moving abroad must inevitably bring about an improvement.

Fourth was *A Less Stressful Pace Of Life* (29 percent). We were surprised this wasn't even more universally selected. Obviously it's an important dream but the figure seems to imply that the most stressed people aren't the ones who opt to go abroad. At first it seems counter-intuitive. But when you think about it, that adds up. Those kinds of personalities can't think in terms of downshifting, or of escaping. Which is precisely why they're stressed. When you note that *Healthier Lifestyle* (24 percent) was fifth and that *Enjoying Outdoor Sports* scored 18 per cent you begin to see that the whole health business is a huge motivation.

Sixth in importance was *A Better Place To Bring Up Children*. Almost everybody who wrote about their experience felt positive about it (see *Children* below).

Just to clarify, the percentages below add up to more than 100 because respondents ticked more than one option.

Dream	% respondents
Top 24	
Enjoying a better climate	47
Experiencing a different way of life	37
Life will somehow be better	32
A less stressful pace of life	29
Healthier lifestyle	24
A better place to bring up children	22

Au Revoir Angleterre

Life will be cheaper	21
Enjoying outdoor sports	18
Making a new start	15
Finding new stimulation	13
An affordable dream home	12
Being near sunny beaches	11
Personal growth	11
Restoring an old ruin	10
Becoming fluent in another language	9
Being near ski slopes	9
Retirement in the sun	9
Romance	8
Living among like-minded people	7
Foodie heaven	7
Becoming a real European	6
Becoming an artist or writer	6
Living in the wilderness	6
Having your own olive grove	5

The other 10

Joining relatives or friends abroad	4
Starting a business	4
Running a guesthouse	3
Having a boat in the Med	2
Playing host to the folks back home	2
Year round gardening	1
Paying less tax	1
Having your own vineyard	0
Living more stylishly	0
Having an open top sports car	0

What people say about living abroad

There was no consistency among the small number of 'other' dreams that respondents volunteered. Some were zany to say the least. One male respondent said he'd moved to Catalonia in the expectation of living in a patriarchal society. Apparently his feminist wife was far too stroppy for him.

Does the reality match the dream?

Most respondents were very pleased with their move. A fifth of those who answered this question even awarded the magic 10 out of 10. And almost two thirds scored eight or higher. That's a pretty impressive approval rating.

Only 9 percent gave a score of five or lower and some of those made the point that their initial rating was low but that it was rising as time went by. One respondent awarded a five but explained that was only because the reality turned out to be not worse than the dream but simply very different. His satisfaction with his new life he scored at nine; it just wasn't how he'd thought it would be. Another respondent, who scored the reality at two, said his bitterness was entirely due to the relationship with his now ex-wife. In fact, in answer to the question *What would you do differently another time* he had even put: 'not bring my wife'.

One woman commented that 'our expectations were too high and too unrealistic'. She and her husband had dreamed of living in the countryside abroad quite overlooking the fact that both of them *hated* the countryside in Britain.

But, in general, the majority of expats found the reality matched their dreams pretty well. Partly this has to be due to the fact that Europe is now very familiar. Millions of Brits set off for their holidays in the Mediterranean every summer and find few surprises when they make a permanent move. Quite likely the responses would be rather different for destinations such as Australia, New Zealand and Canada.

Score out of 10	% of respondents
1	
2	1
3	1
4	2
5	5
6	10
7	15
8	29
9	16
10	20

What would expats do differently next time?

This question stumped just over a fifth of respondents who couldn't come up with any answer at all. And a further 19 percent answered quite confidently 'nothing'.

Of the remaining answers most could be paraphrased into just four categories. Eighteen percent said they should have taken more time to research, plan and prepare their move. Some wished they'd done more research on schools, others that they'd taken longer to choose a house (3-6 months more, one person wrote) and still others that they had looked more deeply into the tax considerations. One respondent wrote that he'd paid too much money for an old property because he hadn't spent enough time comparing prices.

What people say about living abroad

Twelve percent said they should have studied the language before going. This is good advice. People assume they'll pick it up very quickly but, for adults, it just isn't that easy (see *Becoming Fluent In Another Language*).

Seven percent said they wished they'd chosen somewhere else, either a different town/village or a different country. One wished he'd gone somewhere with less hunting. We can certainly relate to this. Round our way from October to February men dressed in SAS style gear blast away at thrushes three days a week (more if there's a *fiesta*). Crazy!

Six percent said they wished they'd made the move earlier. In one case this was for the particular reason that the respondent's children were grown up by the time of the move and refused to accompany her. If she'd moved when the children were young she feels sure they would have stayed and be with her now. On the other hand, the wife in a recently retired couple wished they'd *delayed* moving until they'd first adjusted to life without work.

Do differently	*% of respondents*
Nothing	19
More research/planning/preparation	18
Study language before going	12
Choose a different destination	7
Move sooner/younger	6
Other	16
Don't know/no answer	22

So what's the downside of living abroad?

When it comes to the downside of living abroad, the same problem came up again and again in different guises – *isolation*. Being away from family and friends. Being unable to speak to local people because of the language problem. More than half of all respondents drew attention to this. Only 9 percent of respondents said there was no downside.

Downside	% of respondents
Separation from family and friends	30
Language	24
Cultural differences	16
Nothing	9
Bureaucracy	6
Work related problems	5
Having to make trips back to UK	5
Heat and flies	3

Separation from family and friends

Living abroad *can* lead to a more hectic social life, especially within an expat community. But it's important to bear in mind that the opposite can also be true. One respondent said her initial satisfaction rating was initially only three out of 10 but that it rose to eight or nine after a year. She was so depressed at first at having no friends that she sought medical advice.

That wasn't an unusual case. Several women had similar stories of depression. Women seem to find the isolation more insufferable than men, almost certainly because women are generally more sociable.

Women who had relied upon support networks back in the UK (mothers, other family, close friends) found the adjustment partic-

What people say about living abroad

ularly difficult. The more self-contained couples, on the other hand, seemed to handle the challenge better. The couples who do everything together and find one another enough.

One woman who moved abroad because she fell in love with a foreign national wrote of the sense of isolation after a row. There was no easy way to go home to mum. She was on her own against her husband, her husband's family and her husband's friends. She had nobody rooting for *her*.

Another woman who had separated from her foreign partner wrote of the difficulty of rebuilding her life alone. In the village, her ex-partner was looked upon as being in the right.

Once abroad, single British expats seem to find it difficult to meet serious partners, especially if they want to be with another Brit. British expats tend to go in couples so available singles are a rarity.

Language

Quite a lot of expats saw living abroad as a way of learning the language. But when it came to it, many were taken aback at how long it took them. Fully a quarter cited language problems as a downside. And many found the inability to converse with local people increased the sense of isolation they were already feeling.

Cultural differences

Most people saw cultural differences as exciting and stimulating but a few complained of them. Expats in Italy told us they couldn't penetrate the Italian *famiglia* (family). Expats in Spain said the Spanish had no sense of humour – or, at least, a very different one. A couple who had started a business in France condemned the French as less forward looking and less open than the British. Most of the time, however, people who complained of cultural differences were quite at a loss to define them when pressed further. Our own observation is that when things aren't going well, expats tend to put the blame on 'the locals'.

Bureaucracy

Among the most popular destinations, France seems to get the most complaints for its bureaucracy. Form filling is a way of life there. But take a short trip across the border from, say, Perpignan in France to Figueres in Spain and it's a completely different world. Rules still exist and forms still exist but nobody pays too much attention to them.

Nevertheless, when you're running a business the bureaucracy anywhere on the mainland can seem intimidating, even if it's no worse than in the UK. There's long been a campaign for plain English in official forms in Britain, yet many of them remain impenetrable. Throw in a language of which you have only a basic grasp and the bureaucracy becomes a nightmare. In Spain they've even invented something called the *gestor* whose job it is to act as an intermediary between you and the various official agencies.

Work related problems

Expats who had to seek employment encountered problems, especially due to language. Most contented were those who had worked freelance in Britain and continued to do the same abroad (as photographers, artists, writers, computer consultants and so forth).

What people say about living abroad

Another happy group work within the expat community as plumbers, electricians, builders, gardeners and handymen – many expats prefer to employ other expats because they have no language problems.

Having to make trips back to the UK

About 5 percent of respondents mentioned this as a downside of living abroad. Most people we know make at least one trip back a year and a few go as frequently as once a month. Some relish it as returning 'home' but for others it's like going back to prison. At least the budget airlines have reduced the financial pain.

Heat and flies

Although only 3 percent of interviewees complained of the heat (and the flies) on the questionnaire, quite a few did mention it in conversation. The message is to experience the summer heat before buying.

Miscellaneous

Given the opportunity to say anything they liked a few respondents came up with rather idiosyncratic replies. 'Too many English' was one. 'Too many brothels' was another. A few decided they didn't like the local people. One respondent wrote a long letter complaining bitterly of the dirt, the dishonesty and the lack of reliability. But that was a very unrepresentative comment from someone who, in our opinion, would never be satisfied anywhere.

Couples

We asked couples if they both felt the same about moving abroad or if one was more enthusiastic than the other. In about two thirds of cases partners were equally enthusiastic and these couples did seem to be the happiest.

Enthusiasm	% of respondents
Both equally enthusiastic	68
One more enthusiastic than the other	32

Where partners didn't feel the same, 80 percent of the time it was the man who was the driving force behind the move.

Children

Anyone who has children should be encouraged by the findings here. We asked parents whether they thought the move had gone better or worse for the children than they'd anticipated. We also asked them to rate what the children thought. In both cases the average mark was eight out of 10.

Not surprisingly, young children made the easiest transition. They experienced less homesickness and learned the language quickly. Youngsters in their early to mid-teens had the greatest difficulties. They were leaving behind a culture they had grown used to and friends they had known for many years. They were slower to learn a new language than younger children. One respondent said his children immediately enjoyed the new 'fun' things but, after 18 months (at ages 12, 10 and 8), were only just beginning to settle down with the more banal aspects of everyday life. He rated their satisfaction as seven, but only five initially.

What people say about living abroad

Older children or young adults divided into two camps. There were those for whom moving abroad was part of the whole rite of passage of growing up. Their lives were changing anyway, from childhood to adulthood, and moving abroad was just part of that. Others took the move very badly.

It seems to be a case of what nowadays is known as 'tough love'. Children who were thrown in at the deep end all seemed to have learned to swim pretty quickly. One respondent had sent his seven year old daughter to a Spanish youth camp in the Pyrenees for two weeks, while he and his wife sorted things out back home. It was a baptism of fire because all the other children were Spanish. Nevertheless it seems to have worked – at the end of two weeks she was already speaking some of the language and was looking forward to her new life.

One mother commented that, in Spain, her two girls were able to experience the kind of childhood she and her husband had enjoyed in England 30 years earlier but which – she believes – no longer exists.

Quite often, children who had moved at an early age would grow up to be more enthusiastic than their parents. Or rather, more accepting of the new country as their real home. One couple had two small boys when they moved to Spain from the UK more than 20 years ago. Those two young men, as they now are, consider themselves to be 100 percent Spanish. They speak English perfectly, because of their parents, but in all other respects they *are* Spanish.

And, by the way, one respondent said she didn't have children but the dogs voted the move 10 out of 10.

Conclusion

If you're thinking about moving to mainland Europe then the message from those who have already done it – as evidenced in our questionnaires – is overwhelmingly positive. Those who have gone before are generally pretty contented. If their dreams didn't entirely come true they came pretty close. Even when they didn't, the reality may have been different but it was still pretty good.

The advice from them seems to be to do plenty of research and not to rush into anything, particularly not into buying a property.

As we've already made pretty clear we love living where we do in Spain. And if we moved it certainly wouldn't be back to the UK. Of course you'll experience some problems. And if you watch those TV programmes about moving abroad you may get the impression that to do so is foolhardy. But don't forget that TV programme makers are looking for drama rather than balance. Every little setback has to become a major trauma in the battle for ratings.

Our advice would be to accept problems as part of the whole expe-

Conclusion

rience. Some of our respondents spoke of 'personal growth' and, indeed, that comes from coping with problems and finding solutions. You won't do much growing just lying on the beach. Wherever you live you'll have problems sometimes. The important thing, if you want to make a success of living abroad, is not to blame them on 'foreigners'. It's very tempting, when the roof leaks, to blame it on 'foreign' workmanship. Lots of people do fall into that trap. They convince themselves that roofs only ever leak in 'foreign' countries, that burglary is something that only happens 'abroad' and so on. If you have that kind of outlook you're not going to be happy. But roofs leak in the UK, too. People get mugged in the UK, too. These are problems to do with people. Not foreign people. Just people.

Mainland Europe is a wonderful place to live. It's big and it's diverse and it offers something for everybody. We hope you enjoy it as much as we're doing.

Useful contacts and addresses

To help you with your research we've compiled a list of addresses for useful information. As contact details are always changing we've put the list on a website where it is regularly updated, rather than print it in the book.

For crucial information about such things as tax rates and residence permits we recommend you to go to the original source or, at least, to a secondary source whose credentials are reliable.

We would recommend expat websites as a lively way of learning what it's like to live abroad and for getting in touch with other expats, many of whom will be happy to pass on advice.

You can see the list at: www.whiteladderpress.com.

If you know of any sources you think should be added to the list, or if you operate a website useful to expats and potential expats, please let us know.

Contact us

You're welcome to contact White Ladder Press if you have any questions or comments for either us or the authors. Please use whichever of the following routes suits you.

Phone: 01803 813343
Email: enquiries@whiteladderpress.com
Fax: 01803 813928
Address: White Ladder Press, Great Ambrook, Near Ipplepen, Devon TQ12 5UL
Website: www.whiteladderpress.com

What can our website do for you?

If you want more information about any of our books, you'll find it at www.whiteladderpress.com. In particular you'll find extracts from each of our books, and reviews of those that are already published. We also run special offers on future titles if you order online before publication. And you can request a copy of our free catalogue.

Many of our books also have links pages, useful addresses and so on relevant to the subject of the book. You'll also find out a bit more about us and, if you're a writer yourself, you'll find our submission guidelines for authors. So please check us out and let us know if you have any comments, questions or suggestions.

Fancy another good read?

If you've enjoyed *Au Revoir Angleterre* how about finding out about moving to the countryside? If you're thinking of quitting the city life for a rural existence in the UK or abroad, check out Richard Craze's ***Out of Your Townie Mind** The reality behind the dream of rural living*. Like *Au Revoir Angleterre* this book takes the top 24 dreams of living in the country, based on a survey of city dwellers and ex-townies, and examines the pitfalls you need to avoid. From dreams such as having space and wide views or going for long walks, through to keeping chickens or having a big kitchen with an Aga, Craze tells you how to make sure your dreams don't become nightmares.

Here's a taster of what you'll find in ***Out of Your Townie Mind***. If you like the look of it and want to order a copy, you can use the order form at the back of the book, call us on 01803 813343, or order online at **www.whiteladderpress.com**.

Being near water

– The Dream –

Imagine. It is dawn. The lesser-feathered hoot calls forlornly across the marshes. The tide is out and the mudflats are alive with waders and dippers, catchers and plungers. Just out there, where the little waves lap, a small boat is moored, waiting. It is your boat. All you have to do is slip the oars, cast off and you'll be away, out into the bay, out into freedom. There is a little light mist rising and not a soul around to spoil this perfect dawn on the river; this perfect day by the sea. Overhead a heron glides majestically as it comes in to land light as a feather on the edge of the water where it feeds greedily. You hoist your one red sail and slip silently out into the main channel. You pull the collar of your midshipman's jacket up higher as the morning air is still cold but you feel alive, happy, content, smug. This is the life, messing about in boats, fishing, or just sitting and gazing.

– The Reality –

The dream can sometimes live up to the reality but often it doesn't because the reality has something missing, or has an extra something that we didn't take into account. I once took a young son of mine on a ramble along the sea shore and he seemed miserable and fed up. We did catch sight of a cormorant but that wasn't enough. He finally admitted he was disappointed as there was no music. And it was too windy. He was too used to watching nature programmes on the telly where you did get music and it was never windy.

So what's missing from our dream of living near water – and what's extra that might piss on our fireworks? Well, for a start living near water does mean it is damp. Now that's fine in the summer but come the winter it gets to be a real problem. How close to water you are will determine whether you run a serious risk of flooding. Some areas are particularly prone to flooding, and yet townies often view properties in summer and don't even check. One of our local villages has a banked up river, which floods every winter without fail, and alongside it there is an old terrace of cottages built *below* the level of the banks. The amazing thing is that people actually buy these houses, and then complain to the council when they flood.

A friend of mine had a country house once which had the river running through a culvert underneath it. Yes, it flooded every winter but there were flagstone floors and the water came in through the front door and out through the back door. Upstream they once had a yellow plastic duck race. They let hundreds of these ducks go, each with a number attached to its back. They promptly disappeared under the house and vanished. The organisers sent down a diver but he was unable to locate the missing ducks. Eventually after a week or two one bedraggled duck did reappear and someone was voted the winner. That winter, as the river levels rose, you could hear the ducks bobbling about in the brick culvert under the house when it was very quiet in the early hours of the morning. Quite eerie. Come the spring when the levels went down sufficiently they did all, one by one and very mildewy and decrepit, reappear but there was no one there to see their triumphant emergence into the sunlight once more.

On the Somerset Levels (and no doubt certain other places such as the Fens) the houses were designed to flood in winter. This went on as late as the mid 20th century, until the area was drained. As the

Being near water

weather turned in the autumn, all furniture and rugs were taken upstairs, where the family moved to for the duration. I once read an interview with a chap who had grown up like this. They used to moor their boat (their only transport) to the banisters, and fish for their supper from the landing. It wasn't hugely healthy, but they managed fine. Little surprise, then, that many houses on the Levels still flood every winter.

However, many houses which flood are impossible to sell. In areas where flooding is a worry, houses can sit on the market for years after flooding perhaps only once, many years ago. (Until a townie comes along, of course.)

Living near water often means you gain a lot of fair weather friends. They come down for the boating or the swimming or the beach parties when the sun is shining but you won't see 'em in the winter. (This, mind you, might be regarded as a bonus in some cases.)

We often make assumptions about what we are going to do to live out our dream without taking into consideration that everyone else might well be wanting to live out the same dream. I moved to Devon to be near water – the river Dart – and quite naturally bought a boat and expected to be able to rent a mooring locally. I was told I would have to wait for *dead-man's moorings*. Yes, you have to wait until someone literally dies for a mooring to become available. I bought a smaller boat which I tow to the water when I want to use it.

Oh, and another quick word about keeping boats. The amount of time you get to use them is much less than you would ever think and the amount of money you get to spend on them is much more than you'd ever think.

Whether you want to boat, fish, or sit by the river bank in the early evening, you won't be alone. Lots of wildlife also loves living in or near water – mosquitoes, midges, sea gulls (you have no idea how raucous and destructive they can be) to name but a few. The more boggy or wooded your stretch of river bank, the worse it will be for midges.

Perhaps you don't want rivers and lakes. Perhaps your dream is to live by the sea. Long walks on the cliffs, collecting driftwood along the tideline, skinny dipping at midnight. All of this is wonderful, but there are still downsides. If you live near the coast it can be pretty bleak in winter. The weather whips across, the rain drives at you and the view is grey. Beautiful and inspiring for a weekend maybe, but for months on end? You can't even get from the house to the car without getting soaked and frostbitten. Day after day after day. And the wild weather plays havoc with your garden. All that salt in the air means your choice of plants is severely limited. Fine if you're not a gardener, but depressing if you are.

But living near water is fun, beautiful, cathartic and ever changing. It is uplifting and relaxing, and there is *nothing* – absolutely nothing – half so much worth doing as simply messing about in boats. Whoops – a bit of personal bias creeping in there. OK, maybe for you fishing or sunning yourself on the beach are closer to your watery ambitions. But whatever your dreams of water, they can come true if you're wise to the drawbacks.

I know someone who reckons that the best way to live near water is to live on an estuary. This makes a lot of sense. You're protected from the harshest seaside weather, but you're bound to be close to the sea. The wildlife and the view is extremely varied and always

Being near water

present, and you can boat, fish or enjoy whatever riverside activities you please.

— Pros —

- If you enjoy fishing, boating, swimming in the sea, cliff walks or other water-related activities, they'll be right at hand if you live near water.
- The wildlife and the views are inspiring and relaxing to enjoy.
- You'll attract lots of visitors (if that's what you want).

— Cons —

- Flooding is a significant risk in many properties near water. And, to add insult to injury, insurance can be expensive or even non-existent in high flood risk areas.
- Even if it doesn't flood, it's generally damp. This may affect the house, or you may find damp weather affects your health.
- Boats are expensive, and if you don't have your own mooring you can't assume that there'll be one available nearby.
- If you fish, you may find that you get less time for it than you hoped. And you can't simply set up your rod and fish anywhere — you have to have a licence or a right to fish any particular stretch of water.
- Not all the wildlife is fun.
- Living by the sea can be terribly bleak and cold in the winter.
- Salty air by the coast makes gardening extremely challenging, and many of your favourite plants may simply refuse to grow.
- Living anywhere near water is always dangerous if you have small children, elderly folk or non swimmers. You cannot relax for a moment if the river runs through your property or the sea comes up to your front door.
- You have no control over what other people put in the sea or

rivers. You can't assume any water will be safe or clean, and in some cases you can be quite sure it isn't. In some areas, Weill's disease is a significant risk.

– KEY QUESTIONS –

- Do you want to own a stretch of water, or simply have it in your view? Or merely be in reach of it, such as a close drive to the sea?
- If you want to be by the coast, can you cope with the bleakness in winter? How long is winter in the part of the country you're looking in? Would you be better off a few miles inland?
- Is your dream property likely to flood? Badly? Will you be able to get affordable insurance?
- What are your water-related hobbies? Boating? Fishing? Check out how much these will cost, and whether you can easily get access, mooring rights, a fishing licence or whatever it is you need.
- How do you feel about mosquitoes? Most of us wouldn't cancel the dream of living near water just to avoid midges, but it might put you off buying somewhere right on the water's edge. Perhaps you'd be better off with a house a hundred feet up the hillside.
- Are you a keen gardener? Will you be able to grow the plants you want to near the sea, or in boggy ground?
- Is safety around water an issue in your household – are there children or non-swimmers? This may affect how close to water you choose to be.

And finally...

Just in case you've been trying to identify the language of some of our translations of 'Au Revoir Angleterre', we thought you might like to see the answers. Here they are:

1	Do viđenja Engleska	Croatian
2	Farvel England	Danish
3	Tot ziens Engeland	Dutch
4	Adiaua Anglio	Esperanto
5	Näkemiin Englanti	Finnish
6	Auf Wiedersehen England	German
7	Viszontlátásra Anglia	Hungarian
8	Arrivederci Inghilterra	Italian
9	Adjø England	Norwegian
10	Adeus Inglaterra	Portuguese
11	Adiós Inglaterra	Spanish
12	Adjö England	Swedish
13	Allahaismarladik İngíltere	Turkish
14	Αντίο Αγγλία	Greek
15	До свидания Англия	Russian
16	جنلترا مع السلامة	Arabic
17	La revedere Anglia	Romanian
18	A Reveure Anglaterra	Catalan
19	Kveđja England	Icelandic
20	Do widzenia Anglia	Polish
21	Na Shledanou Anglie	Czech
22	שלום אנגליה	Hebrew
23	Zbogom angleški	Slovakian
24	Tot siens Engeland	Afrikaans

The White Ladder Diaries

Ros Jay

"To start a business from scratch with a great idea but little money is a terrifying but thrilling challenge. White Ladder is a fine example of how sheer guts and drive can win the day."
TIM WATERSTONE

Have you ever dreamed of starting your own business? Want to know what it's like? I mean, what it's really like?

Ros Jay and her partner, Richard Craze, first had the idea for White Ladder Press in the summer of 2002. This is the story of how they overcame their doubts and anxieties and brought the company to life, for only a few thousand pounds, and set it on its way to being a successful publishing company (this is its third book).

The White Ladder Diaries isn't all theory and recollections. It's a real life, day-by-day diary of all those crucial steps, naïve mistakes and emotional moments between conceiving the idea for a business and launching the first product. It records the thinking behind all the vital decisions, from choosing a logo or building a website, to sorting out a phone system or getting to grips with discounts.

What's more, the diary is littered with tips and advice for anyone else starting up a business. Whether you want to know how to register a domain name or how to write a press release, it's all in here.

If they could do it, so can you. Go on – stop dreaming. Be your own boss.

£9.99

Recipes *for* Disaster*s*

How to turn kitchen c*ock-up*s into magnificent meals

Roni Jay

"Methinks 'twould have spared me much grief had I had this cunning volume to hand when I burnt those cursèd cakes." *King Alfred the Great*

It was all going so well... friends for lunch, guests for dinner, family for Christmas. You're planning a delicious meal, relaxed yet sophisticated, over which everyone can chat, drink a glass of fine wine and congratulate you on your culinary talent.

And then, just as you were starting to enjoy it – disaster! The pastry has burnt, the pudding has collapsed or the terrine won't turn out. Or the main ingredient has been eaten by the cat. Or perhaps it's the guests who've buggered everything up: they forgot to mention that they're vegetarian (you've made a beef bourguignon). Or they've brought along a friend (you've only made six crème brûlées).

But don't panic. There are few kitchen cock-ups that can't be successfully salvaged if you know how. With the right attitude you are no longer accident-prone, but adaptable. Not a panicker but a creative, inspirational cook. Recipes for Disasters is packed with useful tips and ideas for making sure that your entertaining always runs smoothly (or at least appears to, whatever is going on behind the scenes). Yes, you still can have a reputation as a culinary paragon, even if it is all bluff.

£7.99

What every parent should know *before* their child goes to university

Jane Bidder

Starting at uni is daunting, worrying, stressful. Not for them, for you. They want to appear independent, but secretly they still want support. So where does that leave you?

What Every Parent Should Know Before Their Child Goes to University charts your route through the new parental territory you're about to enter. It draws on the experience of parents who have gone before you to help with:

- how to fill in those UCAS forms
- changing courses, or even changing uni
- organising accommodation
- what to pack, and other essentials
- money and teaching them to budget
- coping with the changes for you at home
- problems from stress to sex, homesickness to drugs, term time jobs to broken hearts

£9.99

Order form

You can order any of our books via any of the contact routes on page 171, including on our website. Or fill out the order form below and fax it or post it to us.

We'll normally send your copy out by first class post within 24 hours (but please allow five days for delivery). We don't charge postage and packing within the UK. Please add £1 per book for postage outside the UK.

Title (Mr/Mrs/Miss/Ms/Dr/Lord etc) _____

Name _____

Address _____

Postcode _____

Daytime phone number _____

Email _____

No. of copies	Title	Price	Total £
	Postage and packing £1 per book (outside the UK only):		
		TOTAL:	

Please either send us a cheque made out to White Ladder Press Ltd or fill in the credit card details below.

Type of card ☐ Visa ☐ Mastercard ☐ Switch

Card number _____

Start date (if on card) _____ Expiry date _____ Issue no (Switch) _____

Name as shown on card _____

Signature _____